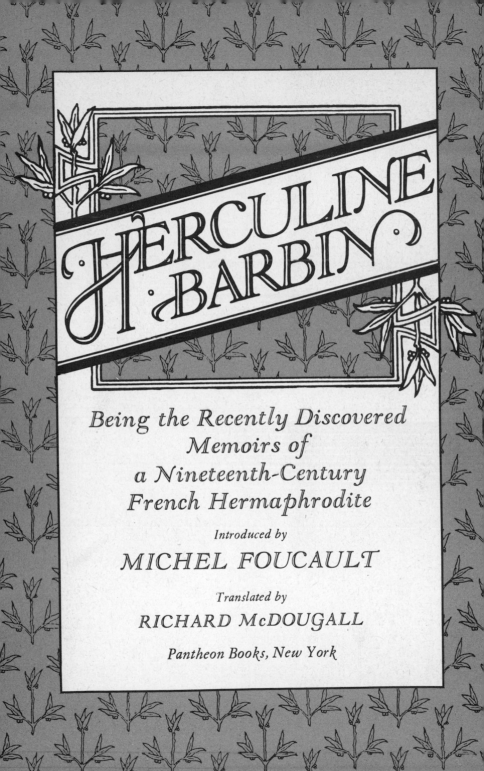

HERCULINE BARBIN

Being the Recently Discovered
Memoirs of
a Nineteenth-Century
French Hermaphrodite

Introduced by
MICHEL FOUCAULT

Translated by
RICHARD McDOUGALL

Pantheon Books, New York

LIBRARY OF CONGRESS CATALOGING IN PUBLICATION DATA
Barbin, Herculine, 1838–
Herculine Barbin: being the recently discovered
memoirs of a nineteenth-century French hermaphrodite.
Translation of Herculine Barbin, dite Alexina B.
1. Hermaphroditism—Biography. 2. Barbin,
Herculine, 1838–
RC883.B3713   616.6'94'00924   [B]   79–3304
ISBN 0–394–50821–1
ISBN 0–394–73862–4 pbk.

Designed by Susan Mitchell

Manufactured in the United States of America

FIRST AMERICAN EDITION

CONTENTS

INTRODUCTION

Do we *truly* need a *true* sex? With a persistence that borders on stubbornness, modern Western societies have answered in the affirmative. They have obstinately brought into play this question of a "true sex" in an order of things where one might have imagined that all that counted was the reality of the body and the intensity of its pleasures.

For a long time, however, such a demand was not made, as is proven by the history of the status which medicine and law have granted to hermaphrodites. Indeed it was a very long time before the postulate that a hermaphrodite must have a sex—a single, a true sex—was formulated. For centuries, it was quite simply agreed that hermaphrodites had two. Were they terror-inspiring monsters, calling for legal tortures? In fact, things were much more complicated. It is true that there is evidence of a number of executions, both in ancient times and in the Middle Ages. But there is also an abundance of court decisions of a completely different type. In the Middle Ages, the rules of both canon and civil law were very clear on this point: the designation "hermaphrodite" was given to those in whom the two sexes were juxtaposed, in proportions that might be variable. In these cases, it was the role of the father or the godfather (thus of those who "named" the child) to determine at the time of baptism which sex was going to be retained. If necessary, one was advised to choose the sex that seemed to have the better of the other, being "the most vigorous" or "the warmest." But later, on the threshold of adulthood, when the time came for them to marry, hermaphrodites were free to decide for themselves if they wished to go on being of the sex which had been assigned to them, or if they preferred the other. The only imperative was that they should not change it again but keep the sex they had then declared until the end of their lives, under pain of being labeled sodomites. Changes of option, not the anatomical mixture of the sexes, were what gave rise to most of the condemnations of hermaphrodites in the records that survive in France for the period of the Middle Ages and the Renaissance.

Biological theories of sexuality, juridical conceptions of the individual, forms of administrative control in modern nations, led little by little to rejecting the idea of a mixture of the two sexes in a single body, and consequently to limiting the free choice of indeterminate individuals. Henceforth, everybody was to have one and only one sex. Everybody was to have his or her primary, profound, determined and determining sexual identity; as for the elements of the other sex that might appear, they could only be accidental, superficial, or even quite simply illusory. From the medical point of view, this meant that when confronted with a hermaphrodite, the doctor was no longer concerned with recognizing the presence of the two sexes, juxtaposed or intermingled, or with knowing which of the two prevailed over the other, but rather with deciphering the true sex that was hidden beneath ambiguous appearances. He had, as it were, to strip the body of its anatomical deceptions and discover the one true sex behind organs that might have put on the forms of the opposite sex. For someone who knew how to observe and to conduct an examination, these mixtures of sex were no more than disguises of nature: hermaphrodites were always "pseudo-hermaphrodites." Such, at least, was the thesis that tended to gain credence in the eighteenth century, through a certain number of important and passionately argued cases.

From the legal point of view, this obviously implied the disappearance of free choice. It was no longer up to the individual to decide which sex he wished to belong to, juridically or socially. Rather, it was up to the expert to say which sex nature had chosen for him and to which society must consequently ask him to adhere. The law, if it was necessary to appeal to it (as when, for example, someone was suspected of not living under his true sex or of having improperly married), had to establish or reestablish the legitimacy of a sexual constitution that had not been sufficiently well recognized. But if nature, through its fantasies or accidents, might "deceive" the observer and hide the true sex for a time, individuals might also very well be suspected of dissembling their inmost knowledge of their true sex and of profiting from certain anatomical oddities in order to make use of their bodies as if they belonged to the other sex. In short, the phantasmagorias of nature might be of service to licentious behavior, hence the *moral* interest that inhered in the *medical* diagnosis of the true sex.

I am well aware that medicine in the nineteenth and twentieth centuries corrected many things in this reductive oversimplification. Today, nobody would say that all hermaphrodites are "pseudo," even if one considerably limits an area into which many different kinds of anatomical anomalies were formerly admitted without discrimination. It is also agreed, though with much difficulty, that it is possible for an individual to adopt a sex that is not biologically his own.

Nevertheless, the idea that one must indeed finally have a true sex is far from being completely dispelled. Whatever the opinion of biologists on this point, the idea that there exist complex, obscure, and essential relationships between sex and truth is to be found—at least in a diffused state—not only in psychiatry, psychoanalysis, and psychology, but also in current opinion. We are certainly more tolerant in regard to practices that break the law. But we continue to think that some of these are insulting to "the truth": we may be prepared to admit that a "passive" man, a "virile" woman, people of the same sex who love one another, do not seriously impair the established order; but we are ready enough to believe that there is something like an "error" involved in what they do. An "error" as understood in the most traditionally philosophical sense: a manner of acting that is not adequate to reality. Sexual irregularity is seen as belonging more or less to the realm of chimeras. That is why we rid ourselves easily enough of the idea that these are crimes, but less easily of the suspicion that they are fictions which, whether involuntary or self-indulgent, are useless, and which it would be better to dispel. Wake up, young people, from your illusory pleasures; strip off your disguises and recall that every one of you has a sex, a true sex.

And then, we also admit that it is in the area of sex that we must search for the most secret and profound truths about the individual, that it is there that we can best discover what he is and what determines him. And if it was believed for centuries that it was necessary to hide sexual matters because they were shameful, we now know that it is sex itself which hides the most secret parts of the individual: the structure of his fantasies, the roots of his ego, the forms of his relationship to reality. At the bottom of sex, there is truth.

It is at the junction of these two ideas—that we must not deceive ourselves concerning our sex, and that our sex harbors what is most true in ourselves—that psychoanalysis has rooted its cultural vigor. It promises us at the same time our sex, our true sex, and that whole truth about ourselves which secretly keeps vigil in it.

Here is a document drawn from that strange history of our "true sex." It is not unique, but it is rare enough. It is the journal or rather the memoirs that were left by one of those individuals whom medicine and the law in the nineteenth century relentlessly questioned about their genuine sexual identity.

Brought up as a poor and deserving girl in a milieu that was almost exclusively feminine and strongly religious, Herculine Barbin, who was called Alexina by her familiars, was finally recognized as being "truly" a young man. Obliged to make a legal change of sex after judicial proceedings and a modification of his civil status, he was incapable of adapting himself to a new identity and ultimately committed suicide. I would be tempted to call the story banal were it not for two or three things that give it a particular intensity.

The date, first of all. The years from around 1860 to 1870 were precisely one of those periods when investigations of sexual identity were carried out with the most intensity, in an attempt not only to establish the true sex of hermaphro-

dites but also to identify, classify, and characterize the different types of perversions. In short, these investigations dealt
with the problem of sexual anomalies in the individual and
the race. *Question d'identité*, which was published in 1860
in a medical review, was the title of the first study of
Alexina; and it was in his own book, *Question médico-
légale de l'identité*, that Auguste Tardieu published the only
part of her memoirs that could be found. Adélaïde Herculine
Barbin, or Alexina Barbin, or Abel Barbin, who is called
either Alexina or Camille in his own text, was one of those
unfortunate heroes of the quest for identity.

With that elegant, affected, and allusive style that is somewhat turgid and outdated—which for boarding schools of
the day was not only a way of writing but a manner of
living—the narrative baffles every possible attempt to make
an identification. It seems that nobody in Alexina's feminine
milieu consented to play that difficult game of truth which
the doctors later imposed on his indeterminate anatomy,
until a discovery that everybody delayed for as long as possible was finally precipitated by two men, a priest and a
doctor. It seems that nobody who looked at it was aware of
his somewhat awkward, graceless body, which became more
and more abnormal in the company of those girls among
whom he grew up. Yet it exercised over everybody, or rather
over every female, a certain power of fascination that misted
their eyes and stopped every question on their lips. The
warmth that this strange presence gave to the contacts, the
caresses, the kisses that ran through the play of those
adolescent girls was welcomed by everybody with a tenderness that was all the greater because no curiosity mingled
with it. Falsely naïve girls, old teachers who thought they

were shrewd—they were all alike as blind as characters in a Greek fable when, uncomprehendingly, they saw this puny Achilles hidden in their boarding school. One has the impression, at least if one gives credence to Alexina's story, that everything took place in a world of feelings—enthusiasm, pleasure, sorrow, warmth, sweetness, bitterness—where the identity of the partners and above all the enigmatic character around whom everything centered, had no importance. It was a world in which grins hung about without the cat.

Alexina wrote her memoirs about that life once her new identity had been discovered and established. Her "true" and "definitive" identity. But it is clear she did not write them from the point of view of that sex which had at least been brought to light. It is not a man who is speaking, trying to recall his sensations and his life as they were at the time when he was not yet "himself." When Alexina composed her memoirs, she was not far from her suicide; for herself, she was still without a definite sex, but she was deprived of the delights she experienced in not having one, or in not entirely having the same sex as the girls among whom she lived and whom she loved and desired so much. And what she evokes in her past is the happy limbo of a non-identity, which was paradoxically protected by the life of those closed, narrow, and intimate societies where one has the strange happiness, which is at the same time obligatory and forbidden, of being acquainted with only one sex.[1]

---

[1] In the English translation of the text, it is difficult to render the play of the masculine and feminine adjectives which Alexina applies to herself. They are, for the most part, feminine before she possessed Sara and masculine afterward. But this systematization, which is denoted by the use of italics, does not seem to describe a consciousness of being a woman

Most of the time, those who relate their change of sex belong to a world that is strongly bisexual; and their uneasiness about their identity finds expression in the desire to pass over to the other side—to the side of the sex they desire to have and in whose world they would like to belong. In this case, the intense monosexuality of religious and school life fosters the tender pleasures that sexual non-identity discovers and provokes when it goes astray in the midst of all those bodies that are similar to one another.

Neither Alexina's case nor her memoirs seem to have aroused much interest at the time. In his immense inventory of cases of hermaphroditism, Neugebauer gives a summary of it and a rather long citation.[1] A. Dubarry, a versatile writer of adventure stories and medico-pornographic novels of the kind that were so popular at the time, obviously borrowed several elements for his *Hermaphrodite* from the story of Herculine Barbin.[2] But it was in Germany that Alexina's life found a remarkable echo, in a story by Oscar Panizza,

---

becoming a consciousness of being a man; rather, it is an ironic reminder of grammatical, medical, and juridical categories that language must utilize but that the content of the narrative contradicts.

The editors of the English-language edition have followed Herculine's system wherever possible, italicizing the feminine nouns which she used in referring to herself.

[1] F. L. von Neugebauer, *Hermaphroditismus beim Menschen* (Leipzig, 1908), p. 748. Note that the printer by mistake put Alexina's name under a portrait that is obviously not her own.

[2] A. Dubarry wrote a long series of narratives under the title *Les Déséquilibrés de l'amour*. For example: *Le Coupeur de nattes; Les Femmes eunuques; Les Invertis (vice allemand); Le Plaisir sanglant; L'Hermaphrodite.*

entitled *A Scandal at the Convent*. There is nothing extraordinary about Panizza's being acquainted with Alexina's text by way of Tardieu's work: he was a psychiatrist, and he lived in France in 1881. He was more interested in literature there than in medicine, but the book *Question médico-légale de l'identité* must have come into his hands then, unless he found it in a library in Germany, where he returned in 1882 and practiced for a while his profession as a psychiatrist. Yet there is something surprising about this imaginary encounter between the little provincial French girl of indeterminate sex and the frenzied psychiatrist who was later to die in the asylum at Bayreuth. On the one hand, we find furtive, nameless pleasures thriving in the warmth of Catholic institutions and boarding schools for girls; on the other hand, the anticlerical rage of a man in whom an aggressive positivism was bizarrely combined with a persecution mania that centered around the dominating figure of William II. On the one hand, strange, secret loves that a decision of the doctors and the judges was to render impossible; on the other hand, a doctor who was condemned to a year in prison for having written *The Council of Love*, one of the most "scandalously" antireligious texts of a time that abounded in such texts; a doctor who was later expelled from Switzerland, where he had sought refuge, after an "outrage" upon a female minor.

The result is indeed remarkable. Panizza kept a few important elements of the case: the very name of Alexina, the scene of the medical examination. For a reason I have trouble grasping—perhaps because, relying on his memories of his reading without having Tardieu's book at hand, he availed himself of another study of a similar case that he had at his disposal—he altered the medical reports. But the most radical changes were those he made in the whole narrative. He transposed it in time; he altered many material elements and the entire atmosphere; and, above all, he took it out of the subjective mode and put it into objective narration. He gave everything a certain "eighteenth-century" manner: Diderot and his *Religieuse* do not seem far off. There is a rich convent for girls of the aristocracy, a sensual mother superior who shows an equivocal affection for her niece, intrigues and rivalries among the nuns, an erudite and skeptical abbé, a credulous country priest, and peasants who go after the devil with their pitchforks. Throughout, there is a skin-deep licentiousness and a semi-naïve play of not entirely innocent beliefs, which are just as far removed from the provincial seriousness of Alexina as they are from the baroque violence of *The Council of Love*.

But in inventing this whole landscape of perverse gallantry, Panizza deliberately leaves in the center of his narrative a vast area of shadow, and that is precisely where he places Alexina. Sister, mistress, disturbing schoolgirl, strayed cherub, male and female lover, faun running in the forest, incubus stealing into the warm dormitories, hairy-legged satyr, exorcized demon—Panizza presents her only in the fleeting profiles which the others see. This boy-girl, this never eternal masculine-feminine, is nothing more than what passes at night in the dreams, the desires, and the fears of everyone. Panizza chose to make her only a shadowy figure, without an identity and without a name, who vanishes at the end of the narrative leaving no trace. He did not even choose to fix her with a suicide, whereby she would become a corpse, like Abel Barbin, to which curious doctors in the end assigned the reality of an inadequate sex.

I have brought these two texts together, thinking they

deserved to be published side by side, first of all because both belong to the end of the nineteenth century, that century which was so powerfully haunted by the theme of the hermaphrodite—somewhat as the eighteenth century had been haunted by the theme of the transvestite. Also because they allow us to see what a wake this little provincial chronicle, hardly even scandalous, managed to leave behind in the unhappy memory of its principal character, in the knowledge of the doctors who had to intervene, and in the imagination of a psychiatrist who went in his own manner toward his own madness.

—Michel Foucault
January 1980

MY MEMOIRS

I am twenty-five years old, and, although I am still young, I am beyond any doubt approaching the hour of my death.

I have suffered much, and I have suffered alone! Alone! Forsaken by everyone! My place was not marked out in this world that shunned me, that had cursed me. Not a living creature was to share in this immense sorrow that seized me when I left my childhood, at that age when everything is beautiful, because everything is young and bright with the future.

That age did not exist for me. As soon as I reached that age, I instinctively drew apart from the world, as if I had already come to understand that I was to live in it as a stranger.

Anxious and brooding, my brow seemed to sink beneath the weight of dark, melancholy thoughts. I was cold, timid, and, in a way, indifferent to all those boisterous and ingenuous joys that light up the faces of children.

I loved solitude, that companion of misfortune, and when a benevolent smile rose over me, it made me happy, like an unhoped-for favor.

My childhood and a great part of my youth were passed in the delicious calm of religious houses.

Houses that were truly pious, hearts that were pure and true, presided over my upbringing. I saw them from within, those blessed sanctuaries where slip away so many lives which, in the world, might have been brilliant and envied.

The modest virtues that I saw shining there contributed greatly to my understanding and love of true religion, that of devotion and of abnegation.

Later, in the midst of the storms and errors of my life, these memories appeared to me like so many heavenly visions, whose sight was a healing balm for me.

My only diversions at that time came during the few days that I used to spend every year with a noble family, where my mother was treated more as a friend than as a house-keeper. The head of this family was one of those men who had been brought to maturity by the misfortunes of a sinister and disastrous era.

The little town of L., where I was born, possessed and still possesses a civilian and military hospital. A part of this vast institution was specially reserved for the treatment of sick people of both sexes, an always considerable number. The garrison of the town, as I have said, also provided at least as many people.

The other part of the house was given over entirely to orphaned and abandoned children whose birth, which was almost always the fruit of crime or misfortune, had left them without support in this world. Poor creatures, deprived from their cradle of a mother's caresses!

It was in this refuge of suffering and affliction that I spent a few years of my childhood.

I hardly knew my unfortunate father, whom a sudden death tore away before his time from the tender affection of my mother, whose gallant and courageous soul tried vainly to struggle against the terrible inroads of the poverty that threatened us.

Her predicament had awakened the interest of some noble-hearted people; they were deeply sorry for her, and soon generous offers were made to her by the worthy Mother Superior of the house of L.

Thanks to the influence of an administrator, a distinguished lawyer of the town, I was received into this holy house, where I became the object of very special care, although I lived among the motherless little girls who were brought up in this pathetic refuge.

I was seven years old then, and the heartbreaking scene that preceded my entry is still vivid in my mind.

On the morning of that day, I was absolutely ignorant of what was going to happen a few hours after I got up; my mother, having taken me out as if we were only going for a walk, led me silently to the house of L., where the worthy Mother Superior was awaiting me; she lavished the most affectionate caresses upon me, no doubt in order to hide from me the tears that were being shed silently by my poor mother, who, having kissed me for a long time, went sadly away, feeling that her courage was exhausted.

Her departure wrung my heart, making me understand that henceforth I would be in the hands of strangers.

But at that age impressions last for only a short time, and my sadness gave way before the new diversions that were offered to distract me. Everything amazed me at first: the sight of those vast courtyards crowded with children and sick people; the religious silence of those long corridors, a silence that was disturbed only by the moans of someone who was suffering or the cries of someone who was dying in pain—all that touched my heart, though without frightening me.

The mothers who surrounded me, offering their angelic smiles to my childish gaze, seemed to love me so much!

I was not afraid at their side, and I was so happy when one of them, taking me on her knees, would offer her sweet face for me to kiss!

I soon saw my young companions, and I grew fond of

them very quickly. For them also, I felt that I was the object of an almost respectful partiality, so well did the poor children understand how much their own lot differed from mine. I myself had a family, a mother, and more than once I excited their envy—as I understood better later on. A childish quarrel arose between us. I no longer recall why one of them, the girl for whom I had the most affection, reproached me bitterly for taking a share of a loaf of bread that was not meant for me. I am passing rapidly over this early period of my life, which no serious incident saddened.

One day when, according to my habit, I had accompanied the good Sister M.—of whom I was the spoiled child, I must admit—on her visits to some indigent sick people of the town in their poor homes, she informed me that I would henceforth be entrusted to the care of others. Thanks to her widely recognized influence, she had managed to have me placed in the convent of the Ursulines so that I might take my First Communion there and at the same time receive a more finished education. My first reaction, I confess, was altogether joyful. The good nun saw that, no doubt, for her noble face expressed a kind of jealous sadness that I attributed, not without reason, to the power of her affection for me.

"There," the excellent woman said to me, "you will share the life of girls who are mostly rich and noble. Your companions in study and play will no longer be the nameless children with whom you have lived until now, and no doubt you will soon forget the women who have replaced your absent mother." I have already said, I believe, that I was particularly fond of the good Sister M., and I could not hear her accuse me like that without being deeply hurt.

I had taken her hand, which I clasped in my own, and,

unable to explain myself otherwise, for I was violently upset, I brought it to my lips.

This mute protestation reassured her about my feelings, though without making her forget that others now were going to have rights to my affection, to my respect.

A few days later I entered the convent of S. as a boarding student. The good Sister M. had chosen to accompany me there herself and put me personally in the hands of the Mother Superior of that house.

I shall never forget the impression I had at the sight of that woman. I never saw so much majestic grandeur and such expressive beauty in a religious habit. Mother Eléonore, as she was called, belonged, I learned later, to the highest nobility of Scotland.

Her bearing was proud and inspired respect. However, a more sympathetic, a more attractive face could not be seen. To look at her was to love her. To a very extensive knowledge she united rare skills, of which she had given proof in directing the affairs of the house. The boundless consideration that she enjoyed in high society had made her an authority in the town.

Others besides myself could declare that she deserved it in every respect. Today, as I write these lines, she is no longer living, and I feel that I shall miss her forever. Her memory is still one of the sweetest that have remained with me. In the midst of the incredible disturbances of my life, I liked to remember the gentleness of her angelic smile, and I felt happier.

I was soon at ease in this holy house, under the aegis of an affection of which I was instinctively as proud as I was happy.

The boarding school was large, and, as I have said, it consisted in particular of girls who later were called to occupy a certain rank in society, whether because of their birth or because of their wealthy position.

Thus, between them and myself there was a natural line of demarcation that the future alone was able to break.

However, I never had to suffer at their hands because of that social difference, which young people sometimes understand only too quickly and which, in imitation of other older children, they abuse cruelly.

They were all fond of me, and I must say that I did not feel any pride because of it, for I believed from that time on that my affection did not have the slightest value in their eyes.

The studies were serious and were entrusted to really intelligent hands.

Gifted as I was with a true aptitude for serious studies, I soon profited from them greatly.

My progress was rapid, and more than once it aroused the astonishment of my excellent teachers.

It was not the same for handicrafts, for which I showed the deepest aversion and the greatest incapacity.

The time my companions employed in making those little masterpieces intended to decorate a drawing room or dress up a young brother, I myself spent in reading. History, ancient or modern, was my favorite passion.

I found in it satisfaction for that urge to know, which was invading all my faculties. This cherished occupation also had the advantage of distracting me from the vague sadness that then dominated me completely.

How many times did I excuse myself from walking with the others in order to be able to walk alone, with a book in my hand, on the magnificent paths of our beautiful garden, at the end of which there was a little wood planted with dark, dense chestnut trees!

The vista was broad, grandiose, and rejoiced in the luxuriant vegetation of southern regions.

How many times, too, did Madame Eleonore surprise me in the midst of that inexplicable reverie, and how her look had the power to make me forget everything! I would run, radiant, to meet her, and rarely did I not obtain a kiss, which I would return in an embrace that was full of an incomparable charm for me.

At times I felt an immense need for strong and sincere affection, and, what is remarkable, I hardly dared to show it.

Among my brilliant companions I had made a friend of the daughter of a counselor of the royal court of . . .

I loved her at first sight, and though her outward appearance had nothing about it that was dazzling, it was irresistibly attractive because of the modest grace that was shed over her entire person; without being beautiful, her features had a charming regularity and bore the grievous stigmata of a sickness that seems by preference to seek out its victims among the youngest and the most fortunately gifted. Poor Lea was of that number. Although she was barely seventeen years old, she already bent toward the earth a brow upon which could be read sufferings that were as yet half-hidden but that were to develop before long at a terrifying rate.

I had surmised that she was an ailing creature, doomed to an untimely death.

Whether or not it was our physical condition that had brought about this closeness between us—which should have been prevented by the age difference that separated us, for I was less than twelve years old—I would be unable to explain. Certain forms of sympathy cannot be explained. They are born without having been provoked.

At this same period I myself was weak and in feeble health.

My condition prompted serious concern, which explains to me certain looks of the good sisters who surrounded me. Like Lea, I was the object of constant care, and the sick ward of the infirmary brought us together more than once.

I lavished upon her a devotion that was ideal and passionate at the same time.

I was her slave, her faithful and grateful dog. I loved her with the same ardor I put into everything.

I could have wept for joy when I saw her lower toward me those long, perfectly formed eyelashes, with an expression as soft as a caress.

How proud I was when she chose to lean on me in the garden!

With our arms entwined, we would thus wander over the long paths, which were bordered on each side with thick rose bushes.

She talked with that lofty and incisive spirit that characterized her.

Her beautiful blond head bent down toward me, and I thanked her with a kiss that was full of warmth.

"Lea," I would say to her then, "Lea, I love you!" The study bell would soon separate us, for Mademoiselle de R. was in the most advanced class. She was an accomplished student, and her stay at the convent had been prolonged for no other reason than to cultivate her artistic skills, in which she excelled in a way that made her teachers proud.

When the evening came, we separated until the next day

at the hour of mass. We spent the night in different dormitories. The one that she occupied communicated with the single dressing room of the school. Thus I sometimes had a pretext for seeing her again before going to sleep. Madame Marie de Gonzague had already reproached me many times for my daily infractions, threatening that she would no longer tolerate my absences from the dormitory.

One evening in the month of May, I recall, I had succeeded in eluding her supervision. The bedtime prayer had been said; she had just gone down to visit Madame Eléonore in her quarters.

No longer hearing her on the staircase, I softly crossed the dormitory, then a big room that was used by the music students. When I reached the dressing room, I took up at random the first object at hand, and from there I went on without a sound to the little room I knew to be Lea's. Without a sound I bent down toward her bed, and kissing her several times, I slipped around her neck a little ivory crucifix of very pretty workmanship, which she had appeared to me to desire. "Here, my friend," I said to her, "accept this and wear it for me."

I had no sooner finished than I started hastily to go back the way I had come. But I had not gone halfway when familiar footsteps made me tremble. My teacher was behind me, and she had seen me.

I stopped at a loss, trying vainly to prevent the outburst. Not having even this recourse, I waited bravely.

"*Mademoiselle*," the good sister said to me sharply, "I will not inflict punishment upon you; Mother Eléonore will attend to it tomorrow."

This threat carried in itself the most terrible punishment

for me. What I felt for our Mother was a kind of affectionate and submissive adoration rather than fear. The thought that I had incurred her displeasure was unbearable to me.

I slept badly that night, and my awakening was painful. At mass I did not dare to turn my head for fear of meeting her look.

During the recreation period that followed breakfast, a lay sister came to tell me to report to the Mother Superior's study. I entered it trembling, like a condemned man going before his judge.

I believe I can still see that serene and imposing face. The noble woman was sitting in a modest armchair while her feet were resting upon a prie-dieu that stood against a wall and was surmounted by a big ebony cross.

"My child," she said sadly, "I have learned about your infraction of the regulation, and were it not for the sake of the good Mother Superior who entrusted you to my care, I would not hesitate to strike you from the list of those who are going to take First Communion this year. I am aware of the affection she has devoted to you, which I have tried to replace in all circumstances."

Then, changing her manner, she made me a sign whose meaning I understood, and I sat down on a little stool at her feet.

I wept silently, my head leaning against her arm, which she did not withdraw.

Then began for me one of those pious exhortations that revealed all the greatness of that truly pure and generous soul. I did not understand perhaps all of its high-mindedness, but today, when I have learned how to judge men and things, the accents of that beloved voice echo deliciously in my ears and make my heart beat faster; they recall to me that happy time of my life when I did not suspect either the injustice or the baseness of this world, which I was called on to know in all its aspects.

I left Mother Eléonore with my heart penetrated by the sweetest joy and the deepest gratitude.

First Communion was approaching, and with it the moment when I was going to say good-bye to the chaste emotions of my adolescence, for I was to leave the community in order to go to Saintes, to be with my mother.

That day was fixed for July 16. It dawned radiantly; nature seemed to be taking part joyously in this festival of innocence and purity.

Twenty-two girls were going to approach the august table with me.

I believe I can say that I accomplished this solemn act in the best frame of mind.

After the Holy Sacrament, which was celebrated with all the pomp that religious houses have at their command, the parlor was opened to all the impatient mothers, who came to hug the young heroines of the festival in their arms.

My own was waiting for me, and she could not look at me without shedding those sweet tears that are the most eloquent manifestation of motherly love.

Our meeting was too short. The doors were soon shut upon her. Not a child was to leave the sacred precincts that day.

The diversions of the world were not to disturb the serenity of those young souls that had just been sanctified.

I have never since forgotten the distressing incident that occurred as that day was drawing to a close.

The moving ceremony of the evening was followed by a procession in the garden.

The spot had been admirably chosen. It would be impossible to imagine anything more imposing than that long line of children dressed in white, as they went down the magnificent paths of that modest Eden.

The religious songs, repeated by voices that were fresh and pure, had something truly poetic about them that stirred one's heart.

The temperature, which until then had been balmy, became oppressive all at once. Heavy black clouds swept across the horizon, portending one of those fiery storms that are so common in that elevated region. Big drops of rain soon confirmed it, and sinister flashes of lightning were already streaking the horizon as the procession entered the chapel again.

In spite of myself, my heart was rent. Was it an omen of the dark and menacing future that awaited me? Was I to see it appear at the very moment I was setting foot upon that fragile little boat that is called the world?

Alas! Reality let me know only too quickly! . . . That passionate storm was only the prelude to those that assailed me thereafter.

I could not eat that evening. A strange uneasiness had seized hold of me. Before going to sleep I had clasped my dear Lea in my arms, and the kiss that I gave her was as sad as a last farewell.

I was going to lose her, too, no doubt forever; for our destinies could not reunite us.

Two years after I left L. I learned that my poor friend had succumbed to one of the most characteristic forms of consumption. Her death was a frightful bereavement for her noble family, of whom she was the idol. Thus was broken the first attachment of my life!

Here I enter a phase of my existence that has no resemblance to the calm and tranquil days that were passed in that cheerful home.

I was at B. My mother had been living in that town for five years. It is a very old city that the great king chose to be made into an important stronghold in time of war and whose name is bound up with great political events.

I am feeling a certain hesitation, for I am about to begin the hardest part of the task that I have imposed upon myself.

I have to speak of things that, for a number of people, will be nothing but incredible nonsense because, in fact, they go beyond the limits of what is possible.

It will be difficult for them, no doubt, to get an exact idea of what my feelings were in the midst of the extraordinary peculiarities of my life.

There is only one thing that I can ask of them: that they be convinced of my sincerity above all.

I was fifteen years old, and it must be remembered that from the age of seven I had been separated from my mother.

I used to see her only at rare intervals. My coming to B., to the house where she was living, had always been celebrated as if I were a member of the family. This time I was returning to it for good. This family consisted of five people.

Its head, a venerable old man with white hair, was truly the living personification of honor and loyalty.

With him was his younger daughter. All the generous instincts of this adored father were reproduced in that proud soul, who bore up against the bitter griefs of an unhappy marriage.

Madame de R. had three children, upon whom she had turned the inexhaustible tenderness that filled her heart.

She had pledged to my mother that kind of deep devotion which does not know social boundaries once it is understood and appreciated. Despite the subordinate rank that she occupied, my mother was a friend in her eyes, a confidante.

Before very long, Madame de R. had only one desire: to keep me in the house by attaching me to her daughter, who was eighteen years old at the time. With my natural pride, I would certainly have rejected such a proposal if it had come from a stranger.

Here the situation was different. I was with my mother in a family that bit by bit I had become accustomed to consider as my very own; so I accepted, to everybody's great satisfaction.

Mademoiselle Clotilde de R. combined with great beauty a certain haughtiness that she forgot only with me. She saw me simply as a child whom she could treat on an equal footing without compromising herself.

So there I was, her *lady's maid*.

Although I did not possess all the qualifications for my position, I always remained in her good graces.

Only a little waiting room separated my bedroom from hers.

I was present in the morning when she arose, and that was always early, in the summer as in the winter. Afterward, I dressed her, and during this operation we would talk about all possible subjects, vying with each other for a chance to speak. If a silence set in, I would innocently start admiring her. The whiteness of her skin had no equal. It was impossible to imagine more graceful contours without being dazzled by them.

That is what happened to me. Sometimes I could not refrain from paying her a compliment, which she received with the best grace in the world, without its either surprising her or making her more vain.

Changing the subject then, she would inquire about my health, which had improved very little in spite of the fastidious care that had been lavished upon me. If I complained about an indisposition, I had to follow such or such a diet. Any piece of advice in this connection was an order that I had to carry out, under pain of lacking in obedience.

It would often have been necessary, even for a trifle, to resort immediately to the doctor.

This man came frequently to the mansion, for my noble benefactor, Monsieur de Saint-M., lived in a state of habitual suffering. Sharp pains kept him almost constantly nailed to his bed or in an immense armchair. Only my mother had the privilege of calming him in the midst of the atrocious crises that shook him.

I had my great and my small ways of entering his presence. I was his reader, his secretary. When his health permitted—and it was a precious distraction for him—he had me meticulously inspect and read over enormous bundles of family papers. "Come near me, Camille," he would say to me, "and see if you can find such or such a letter, pertaining to the matter you know so well." I would read slowly, stealing a glance at him from time to time to see if I had satisfied him.

When the reading was finished, I would still go on looking for and finding fragments of intimate correspondence. For the most part they were letters from a sister or from his eldest brother, a brave general of the Empire, who had been gloriously wounded upon our great battlefields. I was always happy when I made such a discovery, for it provided him with the subject of a throng of stories I would listen to with a matchless eagerness.

Although I was very young, he put a boundless trust in me.

As I have already said, I had read a great deal. My judgment had been developed early. At the age when one still belongs to adolescence, I was serious, thoughtful, and none of the principal facts of our history, which is so rich in great events, was unknown to me.

At fixed hours my young mistress came and sat down near her grandfather, of whom she was the favorite; but her presence did not interrupt the work that had been begun.

When the evening came, I would read the paper.

It always happened that he would close his eyes while I was reading and rest his head back against the cushions. The first few times, thinking he was asleep, I stopped.

He was immediately aware that I had.

"Are you tired?" he asked me, and when I answered negatively he had me continue. I had to read everything, except the serial.

It is true that I did not miss it on that account. Only I read it alone.

I thus devoured a large collection of old and modern works that was piled up on the shelves of a library adjoining my room.

From time to time I caught myself reading to a very late hour of the night. It was my recreation, my relaxation. I acquired more than one useful lesson from it, I must say.

I confess that I was extraordinarily shaken when I read Ovid's *Metamorphoses*. Those who know them can imagine how I felt. As the sequel of my story will clearly show, this discovery had a special bearing on my case.

The years slipped away. I reached seventeen. My condition, although it did not present any anxieties, was no longer natural.

As the days passed, the doctor who had been consulted recognized that the most promising remedies were ineffective. He had finally decided not to worry about the matter any more but to leave everything to time. As for myself, I was not at all frightened.

Mademoiselle Clotilde de R. was twenty years old. It had been planned quite a while that she would marry one of her cousins, who was the heir, through his mother, to a brilliant fortune, and who bore a name that will be forever famous in the annals of the French navy.

His return, which had been so eagerly awaited by his beautiful fiancée, was immediately followed by the preliminaries essential to their union.

Though he was not a model of masculine beauty, Raoul de K. was one of those men who are attractive from the very start.

His open face, which bore the stamp of a naturally distinguished character, made a captivating man of him, if not a handsome gallant. Any woman should have been proud to belong to him.

What I can say for certain is that the pure girl whom he was going to make his wife loved him as ardently as her angelic nature allowed.

Great family festivities awaited the young married couple at the Château de C., Madame de K.'s customary residence.

They went there eight days after the celebration of the marriage, which Monsieur de Saint-M. could not attend, as his condition condemned him to strict confinement.

After having received the benediction of her revered grandfather, that adorable woman kissed me tenderly, making me promise never to forget her in any circumstance of my life.

She was far away from me before I was in a condition to answer her.

This scene had overwhelmed me.

I could not refrain from weeping when I saw again the elegant apartment that my mistress had occupied. An indefinable sensation tortured me at the thought that she would no longer be there to give me her first smile in the morning, her final word before going to sleep.

A change in my destiny was going to take place. I now needed a new occupation.

The excellent parish priest, a friend of the household and my spiritual guide, gave me the idea of devoting myself to teaching. With my authorization, he told my mother as well as my benefactor about it. This proposal pleased both of them, as I had expected.

It displeased me supremely. I had an antipathy toward this profession that was not reasoned but deep.

I was no more flattered by the prospect of being a *working woman*. I believed I deserved better than that.

One evening when I had finished my daily reading to Monsieur de Saint-M., and when my mother, who was sitting next to me, was preparing his tea for him, a portion of which always came to me, I saw them consult each other with a look, as if they were asking who should begin.

He did. "Camille," he said to me, "you have received a good start in your education. You are intelligent; it only depends on you to enter before long the normal school of . . . With your aptitude, you will leave it two years from now equipped with a teaching certificate. No career could better suit your ideas and your principles."

His words had touched me, and I was furthermore struck by the rightness of his reasoning, in which I had an unshakable faith. My decision and my answer came at once. I thanked him effusively, promising that I would justify his good opinion of me.

My mother was no less happy about my answer; she was awaiting it with an understandable impatience, while thinking that this dream at once satisfied her pride and appeased her maternal anxieties for my future.

It was all over. My fate was sealed. That evening had determined the rest of my life! But, Lord, how different it was from the one they were expecting!!

It was without terror that I now confronted the new career I had accepted, for I could not dream of any other. It would be a lie to say that I was happy about it. I was only indifferent to it.

I nevertheless set to work, driven as I was by the ambition to succeed. Who has not felt this feverish ardor just before the day that is to find you in the presence of a board of examiners?

Every year the normal school of . . . received twelve girls from the department. Before entering it, every one of them underwent a preparatory examination that was generally reviewed by the superintendent of schools. Abbé N. had given me in this respect all the information that was necessary.

While my mother was taking care of my school outfit, I was actively at work, and in a few months I found myself sufficiently prepared for this first struggle. The month of August was approaching, the time when the examinations take place. I had long since filed my birth certificate at the office of the superintendent of schools, as well as a certificate of good morals, which had been endorsed by the mayor's office.

It was August 18. That year the normal school of . . . presented about ten candidates for the teaching certificate, among whom was a sister of my mother's. As she was only a few years older than I, I regarded her as my own sister.

Because of her I was already known, both to her companions and to the good Mother Superior, who accompanied them.

The latter thus regarded me as her future student, and she treated me with very special kindness.

I was indebted to her for the touching preference she had for my aunt, who was one of her dearest students and from whom she would not have consented to be separated.

To say that I was happy about the prospect that this career offered me would be perfectly false. I embraced it without distaste, it is true, but also without inclination. And yet at the time I had no suspicion of the innumerable difficulties that surround the most servile of all stations, that of a schoolmistress.

Of course, everyone knows nowadays about the dependent position, shameful for our era, in which the male and female teachers of boarding schools are placed. Exposed to slander, to the backbiting of a population whom a teacher has a duty to uplift, they must also endure the deadly and despotic influence of a priest jealous of his power, who, if he cannot enslave them, will soon crush them under the burden of the animosity he has stirred up in their path. What I have seen would permit me to mention more than one example of this kind. The moment has not yet come.

But what I am referring to here is an inevitable danger. I am going to lay myself open to incredulous laughter, perhaps. However that may be, I believe I am fulfilling a duty when I declare that, honorable exceptions apart, the officials whom I dare attack here are more numerous than I dare suggest.

After the curé of the commune, a schoolmistress has no enemy more terrible than the Superintendent of Primary Education. He is her immediate chief, he is the man who holds her whole future in his hands. A word from him to the Academy, a report to the prefect, can banish her from the whole teaching profession.

Imagine then—as I have seen—a man who has reached the position of Superintendent of Primary Education by means of maneuvers that are more or less Jesuitical. Incapable of appreciating the talent or the worth of a schoolmistress who, only too often, could invite him to sit not in the chair of honor but instead on a bench among her most ignorant students: that is the man.

He will be very careful then not to broach a serious subject; he would fail. He will stick to trifles that outdo one another in being ridiculous, while at the same time terrifying the children in such a way as to deprive them of any possibility of answering, as in fact happens. He then goes on to reproach the schoolmistress with a threatening tone to which she must bow, so as not to be crushed under the brilliant superiority of Monsieur the Superintendent of the Academy.

Imagine also—as is sometimes true—that the schoolmistress is pretty, and that Monsieur the Superintendent has been affected, for those gentlemen may be gifted with a certain perspicacity. That much can be conceded to them. In order not to see herself deprived of the bit of bread that keeps her and her old father alive, the poor girl threatened by disfavor will become more sensitive, smaller before the arrogance of her superior. Delighted to have made a child tremble, he is a bit appeased and he concludes with a compliment that in the mouth of another could pass for an insult. But can one answer Monsieur the Superintendent impolitely? No. And he knows that very well. No more than one can remain indifferent to the promises of advancement that he is pleased to offer.

They have gone into the little parlor. The gentleman is pleased to accept a bite to eat. Here it is no longer a question of teaching; he chats familiarly; the ground is more familiar to him. His honeyed words become more and more clear. After having threatened, he promises, but he also demands, and here his language is utterly significant.

Under penalty of incurring his hatred, it can perfectly well happen that she may be generous in return! ! ! . . .

It can also happen that she may politely invite Monsieur the Superintendent to pass through the door as quickly as possible, and also invite him not to darken it again.

And in that case it always happens that the schoolmistress is ruined. Is she going to fight against a man whose lofty moral standards are proverbial? She is reluctant to do so first of all because that would be to compromise herself without ruining him: so she keeps quiet. From that point on there are vexations of all sorts. Notes to the prefecture follow one another, and in their wake come terrifying reprimands.

If, with all that, her curé is against her, it is finished, she must yield ground. Unable to drive her out, he uses every means at his command to induce families to put their children with the good sisters whom he has taken care to call into the locality.

I have observed such scenes take place before my eyes, really incredible scenes of infamous vileness, of abuses of power too revolting for me to attempt to describe.

It is far from my thoughts to have wished to impair the honor of that hard-working class, and so worthy of interest, devoted to the difficult task of teaching among our country people.

Nobody has been in a better position than I to appreciate their willingness to do good, their incessant efforts on behalf of everything that concerns the moral side of civilization. My only purpose has been to raise a question of public morality.

I was admitted to the normal school of . . . It was only a few miles distant, but this journey was still an event for me. One had to sail out into the ocean, so I was going to find the charm of novelty in it.

When I arrived at D., the captain had me taken to the convent. Its appearance was as simple and modest as the lives of those who dwelt in it.

I do not know what inexpressible uneasiness seized me when I crossed the threshold of that house. It was pain, it was shame. What I felt—no words could express it.

That will seem incredible, no doubt, because after all I was no longer a child. I was seventeen years old, and I was going to find myself in the presence of girls some of whom were barely sixteen. The very affectionate welcome of the good Mother Superior had left me indifferent; and, strange to say, when she escorted me into the class of student-teachers, the sight of all those fresh and charming faces, which were already smiling at me, rent my heart.

Upon all those young brows I read joy, contentment, and

I remained sad, terror-stricken! Something instinctive disclosed itself in me, seeming to forbid me entrance into that sanctuary of virginity. My dominant feeling, my love of study, took my mind off the strange perplexity that had possessed my whole being.

There were twenty to twenty-five candidates for the teaching certificate. Still, apart from our class, the same establishment numbered at least a hundred little girls, some boarders, some day students, who formed two separate classes. An immense dormitory that consisted of approximately fifty beds brought us all together.

At either side of this room was to be seen a bed hung with white curtains, belonging to a nun. As I had been accustomed for a long time to have a room of my own, I suffered enormously from this sort of communal living. The hour when we arose was above all a torment for me; I would have preferred to be able to hide myself from the sight of my kind companions, not because I wanted to shun them—I liked them too much for that—but because I was instinctively ashamed of the enormous distance that separated me from them, physically speaking.

At that age, when all a woman's graces unfold, I had neither that free and easy bearing nor the well-rounded limbs that reveal youth in full bloom. My complexion with its sickly pallor denoted a condition of chronic ill health. My features had a certain hardness that one could not help noticing. My upper lip and a part of my cheeks were covered by a light down that increased as the days passed. Understandably, this peculiarity often drew to me joking remarks that I tried to avoid by making frequent use of scissors in place of a razor. As was bound to happen, I only succeeded in making it even thicker and more noticeable still.

My body was literally covered with it, and so, unlike my companions, I carefully avoided exposing my arms, even in the warmest weather. As for my figure, it remained ridiculously thin. That all struck the eye, as I realized every day. I must say, however, that I was generally well liked by my teachers and my companions, and I returned their affection fully but in a way that was almost fearful. I was born to love. All the faculties of my soul impelled me to it; beneath an appearance of coldness, almost of indifference, I had a passionate heart.

It was not long before this unfortunate disposition drew reproaches upon me and made me the object of a careful scrutiny, which I defied openly.

I soon struck up a close friendship with a charming girl named Thécla, who was a year older than I. Indeed, we could not have been more different from each other in our physical appearance, for my friend was fresh and graceful, and I was not at all.

We were always called the inseparables, and in fact we did not lose sight of each other for a single instant.

In the summer, studies were held in the garden; we used to sit next to each other there, hand in hand, holding the book between us. From time to time my teacher would fix her look upon me at the moment when I would lean toward Thécla to kiss her, sometimes on her brow and—*would you believe it of me?*—sometimes on her lips. That was repeated twenty times in the course of an hour. I was then condemned to sit at the end of the garden; I did not always do so with good grace. The same scenes recurred during the walk. By a strange stroke of fate, I had bed number two in the dormitory, she had bed number twelve, but that did not inconvenience me very much. As I could not go to bed without kissing her, I maneuvered in such a way as to find myself still up when everyone was lying down, and I would tiptoe over to her. When I had finished saying good night, I was sometimes caught unawares by my teacher, from whom I was separated only by bed number one. The pretexts that I gave for my escapades were accepted at first; but it could not go on that way. The excellent woman was really fond of me, I knew that, and this behavior distressed her even as it surprised her. On the other hand, since we were not children, she did not punish us but instead appealed to our feelings.

The next day, therefore, she found a way to approach me alone in the garden; and there, taking my hands in her own, as she might have done with a sister, she made the most touching exhortations to me, in order to call me back to the feeling of modesty that was commanded by morality and the respect owed to a religious house. So inspired could she become with that tone of voice, which had nothing human about it, that I never listened to her without weeping.

I have lived enough to be able to say that it is impossible to find anything comparable to that superior nature. I defy the most skeptical man in the world to live in the presence of a creature so noble, so pure, so truly Christian, without feeling disposed to cherish a religion capable of producing such characters. I will be told that they are rare; I know that, unfortunately; but they are only more admirable for that reason, and if they all do not attain such perfection, who then would dare to demand it of them?

Holy and noble woman! My memory of you has sustained me in the difficult hours of my life! ! It has appeared to me in the midst of my frenzies like a celestial vision to which I have owed strength, consolation! !

As humble and modest as she was truly great, Sister Marie-des-Anges carefully set aside any talk that might confirm what one already knew about her high birth. The daughter of a general whose career was among the most brilliant because of the important position he had occupied for a long time in diplomacy, she had early renounced the future that her name and her fortune promised her in order to devote herself solely to the service of the poor and the sick. Her learning, which was extensive and very rare for a woman, had caused her to be chosen by her superiors to direct the normal school of D. It would be too little to say that she was loved by her students. They all adored her. And so she rarely had the occasion to address even the slightest reproach to us; her desires were orders for us, which we carried out even before they were formulated.

The superintendents knew her well, and so their visits were rare and generally short.

This is the way the studies of the student-teachers were ordered: in the morning, summer as in winter, the waking bell rang at five o'clock. At six o'clock, mass, either in the school chapel or in the parish church, which was scarcely five minutes from the community.

At seven o'clock, study, until eight, at which time the bell rang for breakfast. Classes began at nine. The morning was devoted to exercises in French, style, writing, and geography.

At eleven o'clock, dinner, then recreation for the young boarding students and the day students. It lasted hardly long enough for us to finish the morning's assignments. From one o'clock to half past four we would be busy with mathematics, reading, and French. Some days were reserved for singing and drawing. After five o'clock we were free, but not without work, and I must say that it was not a burden for us. Not a minute was wasted. If it happened that we were ahead, we profited from the time, either doing our needlework or solving some new and puzzling question. Thence came our rapid progress. My aversion to handicrafts continued to grow. I sometimes wondered what would happen when one day I should have to confess my deep incapacity with regard to my students. While my companions were becoming stronger in this form of exercise, I gave myself up to my favorite diversion: reading.

In the summer, when the weather permitted, we used to take a walk by the seashore after supper. The nuns accompanied us but without mingling with us at all. An immense beach, almost always deserted, stretched out along the very walls of the community, from which it was separated only by a rampart. The view was delightful, above all when storms, which occurred frequently on this wild part of the coast, would convulse the terrible element that surrounded us. Upon these arid shores the storms had a truly terrifying character, which cannot be imagined.

I once witnessed one of these horrible scenes, the memory of which has never left me. I have never seen anything like it since that day.

It was around the middle of the month of July.

The day had been oppressive. Not a breath of wind came to cool the air, which was scorching even after nightfall. As usual, we had gone after supper to walk for an hour on the rampart. At that moment there was a sudden atmospheric change. Violent gusts arose all at once, coming from the sea, while at the same time dark clouds appeared on the horizon.

It was obvious that a squall was going to break.

I was in a hurry to go back, because ever since my arrival at D. storms aroused a terror in me that I had not felt until then. Thécla leaned against my arm, which was trembling already in spite of my efforts to seem calm.

They were getting ready to have us go back when I was nailed to the spot by a horrible flash of lightning that dropped down through a gap in the sky and crashed only a few feet away from the place where we happened to be, but without leaving any trace of its passing.

I was terrified. The storm, however, had still to reach its full force.

Around midnight it doubled in intensity. The flashes of lightning followed one another more and more swiftly, making the nightlight that was burning in the dormitory perfectly unnecessary.

Nobody was sleeping. The two nuns had opened their curtains and were loudly saying prayers that were answered by some of my companions.

There was nothing sadder than the monotonous sound of those voices mingled with the swelling claps of thunder.

With my head buried under my covers, I was hardly breathing any more. Unable to hold out any longer, I emerged a bit in order to look around me.

Less frightened, the student placed next to me had gotten up and was approaching my bed in order to reassure me. I had seized her hand when a terrifying flash lit up the whole room.

It was immediately followed by a clap of thunder whose like I have never heard.

At the same time, the window located over my bed opened with a crash. Beside myself with fright, I let out a cry of anguish that, together with what had preceded it, gave reason to believe that a real disaster had occurred.

Before anyone could understand what was happening, I

had leapt over—I do not know how—the bed that separated me from my teacher.

Moved as if by an electric spring, I had fallen prostrate into the arms of Sister Marie-des-Anges, who could not disentangle herself from my unforeseen embrace.

She put her arms around my neck, while I pressed my head hard against her breast, which was covered only by a nightgown.

When my first moment of terror had been allayed, Sister Marie-des-Anges gently called to my attention the fact that I happened to be naked. Indeed, I was not thinking of it, but I understood her without hearing her.

An *incredible sensation* dominated me completely and overwhelmed me with shame.

My predicament cannot be expressed.

Some students were standing around the bed and watching this scene, unable to attribute the nervous trembling that shook me to anything but my feeling of fear. . . . I did not dare now either to get up again or confront the looks that were fixed upon me. My distorted face was covered with a livid pallor. My legs gave way beneath me.

Moved by pity, my excellent teacher lavished the most tender encouragements upon me. I had sunk down upon my knees, my head propped against the bed. My teacher tried to raise it with one hand while the other rested upon my forehead. I felt that that hand was burning me.

I abruptly drew it away and pressed it against my lips with a feeling of happiness that was unknown to me. At any other time she would have reproached me for this familiar gesture, which she never tolerated. This time, she was content to withdraw her hand, urging me to get back to my bed.

Possessed by feelings that would be difficult to describe, I no longer heard the storm, which was still rumbling low. I had left without daring to cast my eyes upon my teacher. A total confusion reigned in my thoughts. My imagination was ceaselessly troubled by the memory of the *sensations* that had been awakened in me, and I came to the point of blaming myself for them like a crime . . . That is understandable; at this time I was completely ignorant of the facts of life. I had no suspicion at all of the passions that shake mankind.

The milieu in which I had lived, the way in which I had been brought up, had preserved me until then from a knowledge that, without any doubt, would have driven me to the greatest scandals, to deplorable misfortunes. What had happened was not only a revelation to me, but a further torment in my life.

It often happened that, after nights troubled by *strange hallucinations*, I would hesitate to approach the holy table. Could it be otherwise? From that moment on, my natural reserve increased a great deal in regard to my companions. A fact that I can mention here without compromising anyone will give an idea of it.

During the summer the students who liked sea bathing would go to indulge in that healthful exercise, escorted by a nun. I constantly refused to go.

For a long time they had been promising us an excursion to T., the most interesting part of the island from the point of view of its location. That day finally came. It was a matter of going at least five kilometers on foot, and as many to return. Only the normal class was to make this trip, as the other students were too young. As there was a religious house at T. that belonged to the same order, we were to sleep there. The prospect of staying over added further to the charm of the walk.

It was August. To avoid the excessive heat, we started on our way as early as five o'clock in the morning. The Mother Superior and two nuns accompanied us. We had to cross a swampy region where the vegetation is nothing less than abundant. Everywhere there is sand, which gives this region the look of the bleak deserts of Africa.

Of course, nobody gave a thought to fatigue; but when we were approaching the dunes, we discovered that the ground was no longer solid: it was impossible to advance over this shifting terrain.

At every step our feet sank in above our ankles, and we had to walk barefoot. A wild gaiety animated my companions. It is contagious, as one knows, and so I did not try to resist it.

That free and joyous laughter did me good, and yet I was jealous of it in spite of myself.

From time to time my brow bent beneath the weight of a sadness that I could not overcome. A constant preoccupation had seized hold of my mind. I was devoured by the terrible sickness of the *unknown*.

The kindest hospitality awaited us at T. The good sisters, who had been notified of our arrival among them in their solitude, received us with open arms.

The entire village was put in requisition and gave us the warmest welcome.

There was a breakfast, consisting of fresh milk, eggs, and preserves, to which we did the greatest justice.

After breakfast we visited the garden.

On the upper floor of the house there was a large classroom that we transformed into an enormous camp bed. The bed-clothes consisted exclusively of mattresses and covers. As it was now high summer, that was more than enough. The heat was excessive. Like most of my companions, I had tried to restore my strength with a few hours of sleep.

I shall leave the reader to judge if it was very deep, interrupted as it was at every instant by the yawns of one girl or the laughter of another. I can still see this scene.

Half-dressed and stretched out side by side upon our improvised beds, we presented an appearance that might have tempted a painter. I am not speaking about myself (of course).

Beneath this charmingly scanty dress, one could distinguish here and there admirable figures that a casual movement exposed to view from time to time.

When I look back to that already vanished past, I believe that I must have been dreaming! ! ! How many memories of that kind arise to crowd my imagination! ! !

If I were to write a novel, I could, by consulting them, produce pages that would be as dramatic, as gripping, as any that have ever been created by Alexandre Dumas or Paul Féval! ! ! My skill as a writer cannot match that of those giants of drama. And then, remember that I am writing my personal story, a series of adventures involving names that are far too honorable for me to dare to reveal the involuntary roles that they played in it.

What a destiny was mine, O my God! And what judgments shall be passed upon my life by those who follow me step by step in this incredible journey, which no other living creature before me has taken!

No matter how strict may be the sentence to which the future shall condemn me, I intend to continue my difficult task.

In the afternoon of that day we visited the environs of T. There is no way to describe it.

The little town is literally buried under an ocean of perpetual verdure, whose deep roots have been multiplying for centuries in mountains of sand called dunes.

An immense forest of pine trees extends along the coast, forming a dike against the encroachments of the sea and protecting the region against the invasion of drifts of sand that, arising to gigantic heights, offer the most imposing sight.

Equipped with a telescope and standing upon the highest point of the forest, called the Observatory, one can make them out in the sunlight like so many silver colossi. We were at least four kilometers from that superb beach, called La Tête Sauvage. For us it was the Promised Land. We were to go there the next morning.

The night slipped away too slowly for our liking.

As the religious house of T. could not contain us all, some of us were sent to the home of obliging women neighbors, who were delighted to offer us shelter. I was of that number. Marvelously clean beds were put at our disposal. Our room had three of them, and there were nine of us. Fortunately, the beds were wide. We were able to sleep in them in perfect comfort, although each of us had only a third of one for herself.

I shall not say what that night was for me! ! !

The day had come and we had to leave.

After dressing in a hurry, we had a few mouthfuls to eat, with some fresh milk.

Provisions had been prepared by the good sisters; they were loaded upon donkeys that had been requisitioned for our big trip.

At the entrance to the forest, upon a little hill that commands a view of the vast ocean, there stands a huge stone cross. Many generations of sailors, no doubt, had knelt upon those mossy steps! More than one mother had shed tears there, remembering her absent son!

It was there, under the open sky, that we went to say our morning prayers. Sister Marie-des-Anges, with that heartfelt tone of voice, that great faith that had mastery in her, recited the prayers. I was kneeling in front of her, and I cannot say what emotion gripped me when I considered her angelic face, which showed nothing but a gentle sweetness that reflected the serenity of her virginal soul. Only the sound of the sea broke in upon the religious silence.

That was a great, a truly poetic thing!

I wept while my companions answered the sacred words!

My excellent teacher, who had been struck by my look of exhaustion, solicitously inquired about my health, fearing above all that I might not be able to make the trip without becoming enormously fatigued. I reassured her as best I could, wanting to avoid any particular remark, any question that I could not answer.

We set out. As on the day before, we had to take off our shoes and stockings in order to walk with a certain amount of assurance, for the sand became thicker with each step and, as a result, more unstable. From time to time we would sink into it up to our knees, and more than one grotesque fall occurred to make us forget the fatigue of our awkward advance.

The heat was already excessive. We quickened our pace,

as we wanted to reach our goal as soon as possible and take a rest, which some of us so badly needed.

We were approaching it. The sand burned our feet. We felt our thirst even more keenly because we were now in sight of the silvery billows of the ocean.

The magnificent spectacle that met our eyes cannot be described; that would take a more talented pen than mine.

It was late. After having rested a bit on the sand, we decided to satisfy our appetite, which the brisk sea air was whetting even more.

We spread our provisions on the beach, and everyone did justice to them. They had thought of almost everything, but they had forgotten the water. Where could any be found in this fiery desert? I devoted myself to the general welfare. Two of my friends accompanied me, and there we went, looking for a spring.

More than an hour slipped by before we had found it. The sight of it made us wild with joy.

I drew aside some plants that concealed it, and I threw myself flat on my belly in order to slake the horrible thirst that devoured me. When we had satisfied this imperative need, we thought about going back. Our return was keenly awaited and was welcomed by real cries of triumph. They tore the precious containers from us with impatient hands, without even remembering to thank us.

One of the students had gone down the beach and was plunging her legs in the water.

That was a sudden inspiration!

All the girls immediately took off their outer clothing and, wrapping their petticoats around their waists, rushed deep into the beneficial waves.

Our teachers did the same for their own part.

The sea was climbing rapidly. The indiscreet waves often reached to a height that one might have wished to save from immersion! What wild hilarity there was then! I was the only one present at this bathing party who was a spectator. What stopped me from taking part in it? I would not have been able to say at the time. A feeling of modesty, which I obeyed almost in spite of myself, compelled me to abstain, as if I were afraid that by joining in this sport I would offend the eyes of those who called me their friend, their sister!

Of course, they were far from suspecting what tumultuous feelings shook me as I watched their carefree behavior, which is yet so natural among girls of the same age. The oldest ones in our group might have been twenty-four. I was nineteen, and many of the others were younger. Several were pretty, though without being gifted with remarkable beauty.

Around four o'clock the little caravan returned to T. Dinner was awaiting us. We were very tired, and we still had a long trip to make before we reached our pretty cottage.

We made our way back quickly enough, thanks to our desire to restore our strength with a good night's sleep. I had great need of it for my part, and, as one may guess, the *emotions* that were tormenting me weakened me even more.

Although nobody would admit it to me, I was aware that my condition was causing anxiety. Science was unable to find an explanation for a *certain absence* and quite naturally attributed to it the kind of languor in which I was wasting away.

Science, furthermore, does not have the gift of miracles, and even less does it have the gift of prophecy . . . For some time I had been under a very special diet. The poor sister in charge of the pharmacy put into it a good will that was proof against everything but which was to be crowned with the most complete lack of success.

Vacation time came and with it the time for the examinations. I took part in them that year. I had been at D. for two years. That is a formidable moment for young candidates; but even though it concerned my entire future, I saw it arrive with total indifference.

We left for B. The Mother Superior accompanied us. She escorted us to the office of the superintendent of schools, who gave us a moralizing speech that was completely equal to the situation. The examination took place in the rooms of the prefecture. They were invaded the next morning at eight o'clock, and the written tests began.

Only at noon did we know the results of them.

Of the eighteen candidates for the certificate, I came out first. I kept this standing until the end, and I must say to my credit that nobody was jealous, because it was generally expected.

My mother was in raptures; but certainly nobody was happier about it than my revered benefactor, Monsieur de Saint-M. The success of one of his own children would not have meant more to him.

It was with a really painful ache in my heart that I parted from my interesting companions. Upon leaving the little house of D. I felt a frightful anguish.

It was like a vague, an indistinct presentiment of what awaited me in the future.

Was I not leaving behind me within those walls the peace, the unalterable calm, that are granted by a tranquil conscience?

Was I not going to have to struggle in the world against enemies of all kinds? And how was I to survive that struggle?

At B. I reoccupied my modest room and resumed my former duties with Monsieur de Saint-M., while waiting for the superintendent to assign me to a position. I was on the best of terms with him.

His kindness to me never failed. He was one of those rare men truly worthy of his demanding position, which he filled to the honor of public education.

A few months slipped by in that manner, when I received an invitation from the prefecture to report to the offices of the Academy. "My child," the superintendent said to me gaily, "I believe that you will be content. I have a position to offer you in a boarding school I know, which I do not doubt will be wonderfully right for you. Madame A. is a person of rare talent, and at the same time her respectability is incontestable. If the conditions set forth in her letter seem acceptable to you, answer her immediately. For my own part, I shall tell her about you."

This proposal charmed me at the very start. I had consulted my mother and Monsieur de Saint-M., who commended me strongly; they both saw in it all the guarantees of happiness that could be desired.

I wrote to this lady, who answered that she was waiting for me with open arms. I was nineteen, and it should be known that until I was twenty-one I could practice only as an assistant teacher. Those are the terms of the law.

As the vacation period was reaching its end, I set out for L., the seat of the canton, which was located at the extreme limit of my department. I arrived there after nightfall.

Madame A.'s mother was waiting for me when I got out of the carriage; she embraced me with an enthusiasm that bore witness to her expansive and very open nature.

It is indispensable that I introduce her.

A widow for several years, Madame P. had four daughters, the eldest of whom had become a nun, at Sacré-Coeur; the second, Madame A., had devoted herself to teaching and, with her youngest sister, Mademoiselle Sara, directed the boarding school of L.

My presence had been necessitated by Madame A.'s marriage. She had recently wed a former professor, who was himself the master of a boarding school in the locality. As she could only rarely leave her husband's house, the young woman had to consider finding a replacement for herself at the side of her sister Sara. Since the latter was not certified, she could not remain alone at the head of any institution whatever. The school numbered around seventy students, thirty of whom were boarders. As always, the domestic details remained in the hands of Madame P., who carried them out with the skill of a consummate housekeeper. Sara and I were to attend solely to the classes.

As she had been accustomed for a long time to directing her sister, who yielded her an absolute authority, Madame A. looked upon my arrival with a certain apprehension. And so, in spite of her mother's example, her welcome was a bit cold, troubled. I felt that she was studying me attentively. Everything, down to my slightest gesture, was subjected to her examination. By the end of the dinner, confidence had been completely established among the three of us.

They had been struck by my sickly pallor. I was questioned in a friendly manner about my health, and Madame

P., going into the most intimate details, made me promise to regard her henceforth as a second mother. Her dearest wish, she said, was to see me on terms of sisterly affection with Sara.

I was very tired; Sara herself took me to my room, which was next to her own. There she made so bold as to kiss me, thus winning my friendship completely.

Once I was alone, I congratulated myself on the good luck that had befallen me. Everything led me to predict that I was going to be happy in that excellent family, which already treated me as one of its members.

We were still eight days from the opening of the classes. Sara had another sister whom I have not spoken about and whom I had the opportunity to see the very next day. Married to a tradesman, she lived on the same street, and so she made frequent appearances at her mother's house.

Comparing her to my new friend, I observed that physically speaking she was infinitely superior. Ebony-black hair framed her face, which was a bit pale but slightly rosy. Her forehead, which was rather broad, surmounted perfectly arched eyebrows, beneath which shone admirable eyes whose expression was extraordinarily beautiful; a delicate mouth adorned with dazzling pearls made of her a person who, if not accomplished, was at least genuinely attractive. Add to that the most handsome figure and an appearance in which were to be read strength, health, and the happiness of a marriage that was still in full bloom, and you will have an idea, albeit a very imperfect one, of the power that that young woman must have had over those around her; the sight of her produced upon me an impression such as shall never be effaced.

Sara's face had neither that distinction nor that grandeur.

There was nothing remarkable about her to attract one's attention. Something ironical hovered ceaselessly about her lips and gave her features a certain hardness that was tempered from time to time by the prodigious sweetness of her gaze, in which was to be read the ingenuousness of an angel who is unaware of herself. Her size and stature were above average, and she was perhaps a bit too strongly built for some observers. With a bit of skill, you might have divined an impetuous, ardent nature that was to be driven to the greatest excesses by jealousy.

Brought up by a mother who carried her religious principles to the most austere inflexibility, Sara was truly pious, but her piety was enlightened, exempt from that exaggerated strictness that she could not help deploring in others.

She was eighteen years old then. Not the shadow of an evil thought had ever troubled the serenity of her candid soul. On that day we began a relationship that was not slow to become a real attachment.

Naturally good, Sara surrounded me with a thousand delicate attentions that denoted a generous heart. I was her confidante and her first *girlfriend*.

We went together to see Madame A. She was indeed a woman of great worth.

Judging by her appearance, she must have suffered a great deal. Although she was barely thirty years old, she appeared to be forty. Her figure was slightly bent, as if a continuous pain threatened her inwardly. Her hollow cheeks had at moments a cadaverous pallor, which contrasted oddly with the resigned calm that was shed over her weary features. Her gentleness never flagged under any circumstances. Her mood was the same at all times. She possessed to a supreme degree that look of grave dignity allied to a charming affability, which together had made her the idol of her students.

Madame P. had a marked preference for her. This daughter was the living image of her father, and she had loved him passionately. Madame A. surpassed her sisters with regard to both intelligence and learning. It is understandable, then, that her mother should be proud of her and so would make no serious decision without consulting her.

Putting her faith in me completely, Madame A. did not trace out for me any plan of conduct for the direction to give to the studies. I had, in that respect, complete freedom of action.

Until then everything I had seen at L. was plainly congenial to me. I had to make an exception in regard to the curé. My position at Jonzac obliged me to go pay him a call before beginning my duties.

I went with Madame P. In the course of this interview, which lasted several minutes, I surmised that this man would be a dangerous enemy in the future. I was not mistaken. He was a little old man with a rather sickly appearance—thin, bony, with eyes that were sunk deeply in their sockets, giving off a gloomy light that aroused terror, repulsion. His speech, which was curt, sharp, and in some way mocking, did not inspire conviction. His smile was false, malevolent. Strange to say, the feminine portion of the place worshipped him, no doubt because of the terrible ascendency that he had been able to bring to bear on their timid natures, which he bent under the yoke of a moral code that was pitiless, disheartening, and diametrically opposed to that of the Divine Master.

On the other hand, he was cordially detested by the whole masculine portion, and he well knew it.

Fortunately, such priests are rare, and one really could not be too thankful that they are, for the glory of the Christian religion, a religion that is all love and forgiveness.

When I had returned to the house, I told Sara about my impression, which did not surprise her too much.

"Camille," my friend said to me, "don't speak like that in front of Mama. You would displease her extremely. In her eyes, Abbé H. is a saint. My sisters gave up his direction a long time ago, to the great satisfaction of their husbands. Their spiritual guide is the curé of a little community near our own. Were I not afraid of my mother's reproaches, I would not hesitate to do as much. But she is intractable on that score."

On the days that followed, I visited the surroundings of the town. Madame P. had a rather large estate there, which was kept in the best possible condition. An indefatigable worker, she supervised everything by herself, without the help of her sons-in-law.

Rarely did the daylight catch her still in bed.

She was absorbed in gardening and caring for her large farmyard and her livestock. There were some extremely laborious things that she did not always rely upon her servant girl to look after. That was her life. Without her toil and trouble she could not have lived.

Did she need some vegetables? If the weather was good, she called us, Sara and me. "Go along, my children. Take a walk to Guéret and bring me back such and such." And we would set off gaily, arm in arm. Guéret was an immense garden that belonged to her, a quarter of an hour from the house at the most, at whose entrance there was a delightful arbor. That was our favorite walk. How many delicious hours we spent there!

This country life held an incomparable charm for me! I

felt myself coming back to life again in the midst of that luxuriant vegetation, in that pure and invigorating air, which I breathed deep into my lungs.

Happy time, vanished forever!

We have come to November 1, 185 . . . , the time fixed for the annual reopening of the school.

On the following day, Sara and I escorted all our students to the Mass of the Holy Spirit.

The church of L. had a gallery, one part of which, in the middle, was reserved for the men; the other, on the right, belonged to us.

The two parts were separated by a construction of boards that was high enough to forbid all communication.

My duties began. I was specially responsible for the most advanced students. Sara looked after the youngest. Madame A. helped me a bit in my tasks. She came to the school regularly every day, for an hour in the morning and an hour in the evening. In reality, I was the head of the establishment, at least as far as the scholastic part was concerned; I had very little to do with the rest of it. Sara and her mother received the parents and settled any kind of business with them. That was one chore I was happy to be spared.

Our boarding students occupied two adjacent dormitories; here again I supervised the older students, some of whom were fourteen and fifteen.

Only a thin partition separated my bed from Sara's. At our feet was a communicating door that was never shut.

Consequently, the same nightlight lit both dormitories.

Once the prayers had been said and the students were in bed, we would often chat for hours at length, my friend and I. I would go and visit her at her bed, and it was my happiness to give her those little attentions that a mother gives her child. Bit by bit I got into the habit of undressing her. She had only to take out a pin without my help, and I would be almost jealous! These details will seem trivial no doubt, but they are necessary.

When I had laid her upon her bed, I would kneel beside her, my forehead brushing her own. Her eyes would soon close beneath my kisses. She had gone to sleep. I would gaze at her lovingly, unable to find the strength to tear myself away from her. I would awaken her. "Camille," she would say to me then, "I beg you, go to sleep. You will be cold, and it is late."

Finally overcome by her pleas, I would go gently away, but not before I had hugged her repeatedly against my breast. What I felt for Sara was not friendship; it was real passion.

I didn't love her. I adored her!

These scenes were re-enacted every day.

Often I would wake up in the middle of the night. Then I would slip stealthily up to my friend, promising myself that I would not disturb her angelic sleep; but could I contemplate that sweet face without drawing my lips close to it?

Consequently, after a restless night, I would have difficulty waking up when the morning bell rang. Always ready first, Sara would come to my bed to give me a parting kiss!

She would hurry the lingerers, say the prayer, and then attend to combing the students' hair. I would help her in this task, but, alas! I did not have her skill, her delicate touch, and so the children would be careful to keep themselves as far away from me as they could.

When this chore was over, everyone would finish dressing. During that time, I would go with Sara to say good morning to Madame P. It was with the greatest joy that the excellent woman saw the intimacy that prevailed between her daughter and myself, and she rewarded us for it with a thousand attentions. She kept for us as surprises all the things we liked to eat.

Sometimes it was a fruit, the first picked in her garden; sometimes it was a delicacy of the kind she excelled in making!

A little before eight o'clock Sara would go up to the dormitory to take off her dressing gown and put on other clothing. I did not allow her to do it without me. We were alone then. I would lace her up; with an unspeakable happiness I would smoothe the graceful curls of her naturally wavy hair, pressing my lips now upon her neck, now upon her beautiful naked breast!

Poor, dear child! How often did I cause a blush of astonishment and shame to rise to her brow! While her hand drew my own aside, she fixed her clear eyes upon me in order to fathom the reason for behavior that seemed to her the height of folly, and must have been.

There were moments when she remained struck with amazement.

It was difficult, in fact, for her not to be.

I had been at L. for some time already. One splendid winter day when there was no school, and wanting to use our free time to good purpose, we thought of visiting a little hamlet about two kilometers away. We left after breakfast. Sara gave me her arm. The students, who were walking in front of us, were enjoying themselves to their heart's content. We came to a little oak wood at whose edge an abundant spring, further swollen by recent rains, flowed over a bed of pebbles.

My young friend sat down on a high mound from which

she could easily survey the whole lively flock. Sitting next to her, a book in my hand, I let my gaze wander at random over the way we had already come, then alight upon my companion. Since the morning, she had been feeling a bit resentful toward me. In spite of all her efforts, I had just drawn a smile from her, which I gave back to her while overwhelming her with kisses. In the movement I made, her chignon became unfastened, and her hair, tumbling down, flowed all over my shoulders and part of my face. I pressed my burning lips to it!

I was violently moved! Sara noticed it. "For Heaven's sake, Camille," she said to me. "What's the matter with you? Don't you really have any confidence in your friend any more? Aren't you the one whom I love most in the world?"

"Sara," I cried to her, "from the depths of my soul I love you as I have never loved before. But I don't know what is going on inside of me. I feel that from now on this affection cannot be enough for me! I would have to have your whole life! ! ! I sometimes envy the lot of the man who will be your husband."

Struck by the strangeness of my words, Sara was afraid; her extreme pallor said as much.

But, as she could only attribute them to a feeling of exaggerated jealousy, which bore witness to my attachment, she did not try to give them an impossible meaning. She pointed out to me furthermore that I might awaken the attention of our students, as I understood immediately. She squeezed my hand, letting me understand that I was pardoned. Still, the calm of that existence, so pure until now, had just received a terrible shock.

We returned to the house in silence.

I was sad, bewildered. A consoling smile from my friend

at times succeeded in making me forget the frightful anguish of my soul! . . .

This mental agony was later joined by horrible physical sufferings. They were such that I believed more than once that I had reached the end of my existence.

They were nameless, intolerable pains that, I learned afterward, constituted an imminent danger. I escaped from it through an unprecedented miracle! I had confessed them to Sara, who imperatively urged me to have recourse to a doctor, threatening me that she would inform her mother about them; but I obstinately refused to do so.

These sufferings manifested themselves at night above all, and they deprived me even of the possibility of making the slightest cry. You can imagine my terror! I might have died like that, without uttering a moan!

Happy about this pretext, which was only too true, one evening I asked my friend to share my bed. She accepted with pleasure. It would be impossible to express the happiness I felt from her presence at my side! I was wild with joy! We talked for a long time before going to sleep, I with my arms encircling her waist, she with her face resting near my own! My God! Was I guilty? And must I accuse myself here of a crime? No, no! . . . That fault was not mine; it was the fault of an unexampled fatality, which I could not resist! ! ! Henceforth, Sara *belonged to me* ! ! . . . *She was mine* ! ! ! . . . What, in the natural order of things, ought to have separated us in the world had united us! ! ! Try to imagine, if that is possible, what our predicament was for us both!

Destined to live in the perpetual intimacy of two sisters, we now had to conceal from everybody the terrifying secret that *bound* us to each other! ! ! That is an existence beyond the power of understanding! The happiness we were going to enjoy—might it not, through some unforeseen circumstance, break out in broad daylight and brand our brows with public reprobation! Poor Sara! What terrible anxieties I caused her!

The next morning found her utterly prostrated! ! ! Her eyes, reddened by tears, bore the marks of a cruelly tormented insomnia.

Not daring under the circumstances to brave her mother's penetrating looks, Sara did not see her until after breakfast. Undoubtedly, I was less disturbed, but I did not have the strength to raise my eyes to Madame P. Poor woman, she saw me only as her daughter's *girlfriend*, while in fact I was her lover!

A year slipped by in that manner!

Indeed, I saw it very well, the future was dark! Sooner or later I would have to break with a kind of life that was no longer mine. But, alas! how was I to get out of that frightful maze? Where would I find the strength to declare to the world that I was usurping a place, a title, that human and divine laws forbade me? That was enough to cloud a mind more solid than my own. From that moment on, I did not leave Sara day or night! . . . We had had the sweet dream of belonging to each other forever, in the presence of heaven, that is to say, through marriage.

But what a great distance there was between the planning and the execution of it!

Our delirious imagination had given birth to all kinds of plans, each one more bizarre than any of the others. More than once I had thought of flight as the only solution. Sara accepted the idea, then very quickly rejected it, with terror. My letters to my mother visibly showed the effects of my constant preoccupation. Without making any avowals to her, I prepared her bit by bit for an inevitable catastrophe. They were so many unsolvable riddles for her. She came to the point of believing that I was mad and begged me to put an end to her cruel uncertainties. I tried then to calm her, but I only threw her into new perplexities. What I dreaded above all was that the ignorance in which she found herself might drive her to ask Madame P. for explanations. All would have been lost.

Understandably, my relations with Sara were full of incessant dangers with regard to our students.

Although our intimacies could not be suspected, it was necessary for us to remain within the limits of a reserve that was difficult to keep up, for me above all! . . .

Often, in the middle of classes, Sara would electrify me with a smile. I should have liked to take her in my arms, but it was necessary to restrain myself!

I did not go near her without giving her either a kiss or an expressive squeeze of the hand.

Every summer evening we used to take a stroll in the neighborhood with the students.

My friend would give me her arm. We would come to a field. Sitting on the grass at her knees, not taking my eyes off her, I lavished upon her the most tender names, the most passionate caresses . . .

Indeed, could an invisible witness have been present at this scene, he would have been strangely surprised by my words, even more by my gestures!

A few steps away, our students were indulging in their joyful play. Placed in such a way as to watch over all their movements, we were at the same time sheltered from their looks! We would go back in the same order still. It sometimes happened that we would meet along our way either Monsieur the Mayor or the Doctor, an intimate friend of the household who, having known Sara from her birth, had a real affection for her. He would greet us then in a most gracious manner, pleasing us very much. Just imagine!

Considering how unusual my position at L. was, you can form an idea of the terms I was on with the curé. That was a terrible position! !

In that family, the most respectable in the locality, I occupied an excessively delicate post, one of trust. I had a total, an absolute authority; in addition, all the members of the family had given me their sincere affection, of which I received new proofs every day! And yet I was betraying them. That sweet girl, who had become my companion, my sister—I had made my *mistress*! ! !

Ah, well! I appeal here to the judgment of my readers in time to come. I appeal to that feeling that is lodged in the heart of every son of Adam. Was I guilty, criminal, because a gross mistake had assigned me a place in the world that should not have been mine?

I loved with an ardent, sincere love a child who loved me with all the passion of which she was capable! But, I shall be told, even though a mistake had been made, you should have revealed it instead of taking advantage of it like that. I urge those who think so to please consider carefully the difficulty of the situation.

A confession, no matter how prompt it might have been, could not have saved me from a scandal whose consequences would necessarily have been disastrous to everyone around me. But even though I was able to keep up appearances for a more or less long period of time, I could not conceal the truth behind them from the man who, here below, occupies the place of God—the confessor; and he had to listen to such enormities without being able to break the strict silence that his sacred character imposed upon him. I had to deal with precisely the most intolerant man in the world! The mere thought of confronting his wrath froze me with terror. You can imagine how sarcastically violent he was when I confessed my weaknesses to him!

It was not pity that I inspired in him; it was horror, a vindictive horror.

Instead of words of peace, he heaped scorn and insults upon me! There was nothing in that man but dryness of heart! Pardon fell grudgingly from those lips that had been made to stream forth the inexhaustible gifts of Christian charity, that very great charity whose source is the soul of the One who reveals the Gospel to us, raising the sinful and repentant woman from the dust!

I had gone there profoundly humbled; I left with an embittered heart, completely resolved to break now with such a guide, whose unspeakable moral code was at best fit to estrange a weak and ignorant person from goodness.

What I have said here is unfortunately only too true. But I am in a position to declare, to the glory of the Catholic clergy, that he is perhaps a unique exception among its members.

The false, exceptional situation in which I found myself made me feel this ferocious inflexibility all the more, because I had the greatest need of indulgence.

In fact, to the great astonishment of Madame P., I suddenly abandoned Abbé H.; her surprise became dissatisfaction when she saw Sara do as much for her own part. However, because of me, she resigned herself to it more easily.

People had at first admired the intimacy that had been

established between Sara and myself, and then had criticized it, as being a bit exaggerated, not to say suspect. Undoubtedly, they were a hundred miles from the truth.

For lack of knowing it, they made all kinds of unfavorable comments, and at last some charitable busybodies, as are always to be found, believed it was their duty to warn Madame P. in the name of morality, which had been outraged by our daily behavior in the presence of our students. I above all was gravely censured. They made a crime out of the fact that I kissed Mademoiselle Sara too often.

We noticed, in fact, that we were the object of serious scrutiny on the part of the children, some of whom were rather old.

If they saw me lean toward my friend and take her in my arms, they turned their heads away with embarrassment, as if they were afraid of seeing us blush. The boarding students above all, who were present when we got up, when we went to bed, more than once showed their astonishment at certain little details by which they had no doubt been struck. They evidently talked about them. Thence came the rumors that were spread in public. Madame P., who feared for the reputation of her house above everything else, was seriously affected by them.

Not daring to talk to me about them, she summoned her daughter. "Sara," she said to her, "I must ask you to be more reserved in the future in your relations with Mademoiselle Camille. You are very fond of each other, and for my part I am very happy that you are; but there are proprieties that must be observed, even among *girls*." This bold beginning made us tremble for the future. What would it be like when she knew the truth! ! !

We nonetheless continued to share the same bed! ! ! That

we did so had not entered into the admonitions of Madame P., who was unaware of it. And furthermore, she was not about to suspect us. The excellent woman was too sincerely virtuous and trusted us too blindly to fix her thought on such ideas. More clear-sighted than she, her two eldest daughters, both of them married, were not, I believe, as indulgent in regard to us. Still, they never said a word to accuse me; their dealings with me were always affectionately polite. Nevertheless, I thought I saw that their curiosity was on the alert.

From time to time Madame P. held family reunions to which I was invariably invited. "My children," she would say to us, "the boarding students will dine a bit earlier this evening; as for you, you will eat upstairs."

If I had refused, Sara would have done the same; Madame P. knew that very well. These reunions consisted exclusively of my friend's sisters and their husbands. The latter liked Sara a great deal, while they seemed on the contrary to be ill at ease with me. How is that to be explained? . . . This uneasiness was barely perceptible; one would have had to be *me* in order to guess it. There were always endless polite attentions on their part, perpetual allusions to the marriage of their young sister-in-law. She accepted everything with an apparent gaiety of which I alone had the secret.

Always placed next to me, she would then on the sly cast me a look that was unimportant to everybody but myself! ! ! I always found a means of answering it! In short, this constraint weighed horribly upon us and spoiled our happiness!

The role that necessity imposed upon me sometimes caused me a kind of remorse. I would silence it in order to support my poor Sara, who was crushed beneath the weight of shame! Dear and ingenuous child! Does her behavior need an excuse? . . . Could she refuse the lover that tenderness of feeling she had devoted to the *girlfriend*, to the *sister*? And if that naïve love became passion, what was to be blamed if not fate?

In our deliciously intimate conversations, she took pleasure in using masculine qualifiers for me, qualifiers which would later suit my official status. "*Mon cher* Camille, I love you so much! ! ! Why did I meet you if this love was to become the sorrow of my whole life? ! !"

The school year was reaching its end.

The hour of separation was to come when the vacation period began. Two months far away from Sara, that was a very long time! ! ! And so it was agreed that I would return to L. two weeks before classes opened. Madame P. herself made me promise to do so. Poor mother! ! ! . . .

She too regretted my leaving! I was her second daughter! "Now, *Mademoiselle* Camille," she said to me one day, "Sara is going to be very lonely without you! Spend these vacation days with us. A stay in the country has so many attractions at this time of the year! The grape harvest is coming; that will be one more diversion for both of you." My refusal did not offend her, for she understood very well that my first duty was to my mother. She did not know how tempting her offers were and what a sacrifice I imposed upon myself by rejecting them!

The distribution of the prizes took place on August 20. The next day not one boarding student remained. So we left the dormitory in order to take possession of the little room reserved for Sara in the main part of the building, which her mother occupied; Madame P. lived on the ground floor.

It was a great pleasure for us to be able to enjoy in complete freedom the final moments of happiness that preceded our separation.

They passed, alas! very rapidly . . .

Although it was modest, our little room in our eyes was a palace that we would not have exchanged for all the treasures in the world! There was no more waking bell to disturb the sweet dream of the night! ! ! We used to get up late!

Sara would sleep in the morning, her head resting on my arm! Her beautiful hair flowed gracefully over her naked shoulders! I would watch her thus, holding my breath, sunk in blissful contemplation! ! !

My God! You had given me an immense amount of happiness! Ought I to complain if, in the midst of the deep night that surrounds me, only gleams of that luminous past bring me a little solace in my long misfortune! The twenty-seventh arrived. That day had been fixed for my departure. We got up early. Madame P. had come to wake us.

When I went downstairs I found that she had prepared breakfast; I could not touch it.

Sara came and went, hastily brushing away furtive tears while at the same encouraging me with a wan smile. In spite of me, her mother had got up provisions for my trip that were enough for a whole family.

I let her do it!

I felt a frightful heartache at the sight of those hospitable walls, from which I was going to part for the first time!

This scene was breaking me down, and I had to cut it short. I approached Madame P. "Now, my dear *daughter*," the excellent woman said to me, "think of us, and come back as quickly as you can." All I could do was kiss her without answering.

I had to take a rather long walk across the fields in order to reach the highway, where I was to catch the carriage when it passed. Sara accompanied me; our grief was over-flowing.

I took her arm, which she had passed under my own, and pressed it hard against my breast! ! ! For the twentieth time at least we promised to write to each other regularly every week.

The carriage came; I started off, leaving far behind me a little rise in the ground that hid my friend from sight. It seemed to me that I was leaving my native land forever! ! !

In the evening I was at B. For the first time I was almost sad when I saw again that house where my mother and my noble benefactor were awaiting me, two hearts that loved me so much! According to my custom, I kissed Monsieur de Saint-M., who was struck by the change that had been brought about in my appearance. My whole person showed a noticeable improvement. I had observed it before him, and only I knew the causes of it . . .

There was no lack of diversions for me at B.

I had to see a crowd of people.

All that seemed insipid to me now.

I was pursued by a constant idea.

A new horizon was opening to me in a future that could no longer be far away! ! !

Before leaving L. I had received a letter from Sister Marie-des-Anges. My former teacher invited me to D. to take part in an annual retreat that was held for the former students of the normal school. I promised myself definitely not to miss it. I had a serious motive for going. What words could give a faithful account of my impressions when I crossed the threshold of that blessed sanctuary where I had lived for so many days! I was returning to it after barely eighteen months of absence! But how many events had taken place in that short space of time! ... How many things seemed to forbid me to enter that house in which innocence and chastity lived!

The first face I saw was my good teacher's. It had not undergone any change. It still had the very same serenity, the very same expression of chaste and resigned grandeur. When my name was announced, she rushed up to me with that divine smile that bore witness to her joy and spontaneously reached out to me with both her hands. I drew them to my lips! ! !

The noble woman thanked me in simple and affectionate terms for having answered her call.

More than forty teachers, all of them her students, had hastened from various points to renew their strength with a few days of devout solitude. As the vacation period was on, the whole house was at our disposal. Many of the women were unknown to me; others, on the contrary, were my own age and had been my classmates.

I was infinitely joyful to see them again.

A missionary monk preached the sermons of the retreat, the exercises of which took place in the convent of the chapel, a sacred refuge, which I was no doubt seeing again for the last time! ! ! ...

I had need of that religious calm in the midst of the ever-increasing disturbances of my life!

At the moment when I was perhaps putting an insurmountable barrier between the past and the future, I had need of meditation in the presence of God! ! !

My plan was to unburden myself quite frankly to this unknown confessor and to await his judgment! You can imagine the astonishment, the stupefaction, that my strange confession caused him! ! ! . . .

I had finished. He kept silent, full of thought. My failures, my troubles, had aroused only his most gentle commiseration.

In setting him up as my judge, I had put my destiny in his hands, as it were. "My child," he said to me, "the situation is extremely grave and demands serious reflection. I cannot, at this very moment, trace out a line of conduct for you. Come back tomorrow, and in two days I shall be able to give you my opinion."

My anxiety was great. I felt that my existence hung on the words that he had promised! I did not sleep, or I slept badly. The time set aside for waiting had elapsed. This is the advice that the abbé gave me: "I shall not tell you," he said to me, "what you know as well as I do, that is to say, you are here and now entitled to call yourself a man in society. Certainly you are, but how will you obtain the legal right to do so? At the price of the greatest scandals, perhaps. However, you cannot keep your present position, which is so full of danger. And so, the advice I am giving you is this: withdraw from the world and become a nun; but be very careful not to repeat the confession that you have made to me, for a convent of women would not admit you. This is the only course that I have to propose to you, and believe me, accept it."

I went away without promising anything, as I was not prepared for such an outcome.

He had proposed that I avoid a possible scandal in a way that would only create for myself an even more dangerous situation, which would have to end in an inevitable scandal. On the other hand, I did not have the slightest liking for the monastic life. A feeling that was too strong held me elsewhere. I was resolved to do anything rather than break it. In this state of affairs, I decided to await events.

The following day I left D. On parting company with my dear teacher I was very much convinced that I was not to see her again, at least not under the same circumstances! And so, everything was at an end between her and me! An abyss was going to separate us! This thought saddened me more than any other.

I can still see her angelic gaze fixed upon mine, while my hands clasped hers! ! !

My God! What if she had been able to read into my soul! !

I offered my brow to her lips, which were so pure, then pressed my own upon her cheek! ! ! It was all over! I had broken forever with the sweet ties of my past! ! !

When I arrived at B. I was extremely careful to avoid any occasion for a special interview, either with my mother or with Monsieur de Saint-M., whose touching solicitude did not fail me.

After his breakfast I would read the newspaper to him and put his business papers in order.

We would chat familiarly, with that freedom which is born of reciprocal trust and esteem.

Then I would go and write down my intimate thoughts of each day, my impressions, my regrets; they were all intended for Sara, who for her own part sent me regularly once a week a long letter that I devoured in the silence of my nights. In every one of these missives she urged me to shorten the time that I was spending so far away from her! It was the middle of October. I had promised Madame P. that I would get back around that time, and I was anxious above all to keep my promise. How much longer was I to live in her house? I did not know. An explosion might occur at any moment. I was resigned to it in advance. The closer the crisis came, the more I felt my strength increase! But Sara!

The carriage service had been changed. This time I did not arrive at L. until almost the middle of the night. I was no longer expected at that hour. Madame P. was in bed. She embraced me heartily and wanted to get up to prepare something for me to eat, but I absolutely refused to let her do so.

"Then," she said to me, "go and rest right away. Sara has gone to bed and no doubt she is sleeping. You are going to give her a pleasant surprise." I did not need to be told twice. My young friend had recognized my voice.

She was waiting for me with open arms! ! !

We hardly slept at all that night! ! ! . . .

Happiness took the place of sleep for us, for long hours! We had so many things to tell each other! ! ! As a result, we were still in bed at a very late hour the next morning!

Madame P. drew apart our curtains a bit and scolded us in a friendly way for our laziness.

I wanted to answer in the same tone; but in reality I was troubled. After her mother left, Sara made a disclosure to me that overwhelmed me!—Tears were suffocating her! If her fears were well founded, we were lost, both of us! A real sword of Damocles was hanging over our heads!

Sara feared her mother as much as she respected her. The idea of having to blush in her presence was insupportable to her. I sometimes pictured to myself what that mother's anger, her fury, her indignation, would be upon learning about her daughter's shame! And that under circumstances impossible to foresee! I confess that even while I dreaded such an event,

I prayed for it with all my heart. When it came, nothing could stand in the way of my marriage to Sara! But how many bitter reproaches I would have to endure . . .

Nothing unusual marked the first months of that second year. The monotony of our existence at L. was broken only by the mysterious sorrows of a love that was hidden from everyone, escaping all human conjectures.

I no longer had any kind of relations with the curé. That man was hateful to me!

Although he frequently visited Madame P., he refrained from entering the classroom.

I could not doubt that only my presence prevented him from doing so. He avoided speaking to me even on the slightest occasions.

I congratulated myself for that, as I would perhaps not have had the strength to moderate my antipathy.

I had given him up; Sara in turn had imitated me. I knew about his deep spitefulness.

He might, at a given moment, become a terrible enemy and take vengeance for my contempt. He was on the watch for that moment, as I understood.

To make up to himself for our silence toward him, he had invented a form of espionage, the most painful of all. The majority of our students confessed to him. Not content to ask them a host of personal questions that were more or less out of place with regard to children as young as they, he adroitly succeeded in having them give him a detailed account of all our activities. Incapable of escaping this in-quisition, the poor children would confess everything and would inform us afterward. I shall refrain here from giving a name to such an act! ! ! . . .

Here I must report an event that attracted attention to our

house. One morning there arose a rumor that put the population of L. in a flutter. They had just learned, at one and the same time, about the pregnancy and the confinement of a girl who was barely fourteen years old; the astonishment was at its height. This girl had been our student. She was not known to have any kind of relations that might disclose the name of the father.

The house that she and her parents lived in almost adjoined our own, so we saw her often. When she heard this news, Madame P. raised an outcry. She had a fierce and sometimes ridiculous touchiness about such matters.

Being led astray by passion found no excuse in her soul, which had been dried up by the abbé's narrow moral code.

It is understandable that this incident was calculated to make me think seriously about the probable consequences of my intimacy with Sara. The girl's behavior added to the effect that had been produced by this event. She unremittingly refused to name the culprit; her obstinacy could not be overcome. The doctor who attended her had known her from her birth; he tried in vain to get her to make an admission. It was all to no avail! ! !

"The father of the child," she said to the doctor, "was a traveling salesman." The identification was rather vague, but the family had to be satisfied with it. A short time afterward, she left the locality with her father and mother.

A change was about to take place in my friend's family. Her sister, Madame A., was going to leave with her husband, who had been called to new duties in a neighboring department. Her leaving was a real grief for her mother, of whom she was the idol. At the same time, it caused a serious difficulty, for although I was in reality the head of the school,

Madame A. always had the responsibility for it with regard to the Academy.

I was not yet of age, and consequently I could not assume the actual management of the institution without special authorization. Madame P. talked with me at length on the subject. She dreamed of turning her establishment over to me one day. I did not oppose her on that score. I saw the day approaching when all her plans would collapse by themselves! ! ! . . .

For the time being, however, I had to accept her proposals.

It was a matter of my asking the superintendent of schools for authorization to succeed Madame A. as the headmistress, until the not far distant time when I would be able to bear this title officially. As I have said, the superintendent was perfectly disposed in my favor, and so a refusal on his part was not probable. In addition, Monsieur-de Saint-M.'s influence assured me of the prefect's support. In fact, I obtained it; my request was approved, to Madame P.'s very great joy.

Madame A. left with her husband around the middle of the winter; she was missed by all of us.

Some time later I began to feel again the pains I had already suffered; they were more frequent now, more intense. Sara was worried about them and went on insisting that I see a doctor. For nothing in the world would I have consented to do so; the violence of the attack was such that I had to resign myself to it.

Informed by her daughter, Madame P. sent for Doctor T. I have not forgotten this visit; every minor detail is still vivid in my mind. It was close to six o'clock in the evening. The lamps had not yet been lit. The room in which I found myself with the doctor was plunged in a half-light, which I did not complain about.

The answers that I gave to his questions bewildered rather than enlightened him. He wanted to examine me. As it is known, a doctor enjoys certain privileges with a sick person that nobody dreams of contesting. During this operation, I heard him sighing, as if he were not satisfied with what he had found. Madame P. was there, waiting for a word.

I too was waiting, but in an entirely different frame of mind.

Standing near my bed, the doctor considered me attentively, full of interest, while giving vent to muffled exclamations of this sort: "My God! Is it possible?"

I understood by his gestures that he would have liked to prolong this examination until the truth sprang to light! ! ! . . .

He raised my cover. My disordered clothes revealed the upper part of my body! Uncertain, trembling, the doctor's hand wandered over it, down to my abdomen, the site of my trouble. In his exploration, he no doubt pressed upon the spot, for I gave a piercing shriek, at the same time pushing him vigorously away.

He sat down then near me, gently insisting that I gather my courage; no doubt he needed some himself. His face was distorted, betraying extraordinary excitement. "I beg you to leave me alone," I said to him. "You are killing me!"

"*Mademoiselle*," he answered, "I'm asking you for just one minute, and it will be finished." His hand was already slipping under my sheet and coming to a stop at the sensitive place. It pressed upon it several times, as if to find there the solution to a difficult problem. It did not leave off at that point! ! ! He had found the explanation that he was looking for! But it was easy to see that it exceeded all his expectations!

The poor man was in a state of terrible shock! Sentences escaped from his throat by fits and starts, as if he were afraid to let them out. I wished he were a hundred feet under the ground!

Madame P. understood absolutely nothing. Out of pity for me, she insisted on shortening this fatiguing scene by hurrying the doctor away.

"Good-bye, *mademoiselle*," he said to me with a half-smile. "*We shall see each other again! ! !*"

I got up immediately and went to join Sara, who was busy in the study. She questioned me with a look. In a few words I informed her about what had happened.

At dinner I remarked that Madame P. was more serious than usual. She did not know how to dissemble her feelings; her preoccupation, her perplexity, were visible. At the end of the meal I went to warm myself for a moment in the kitchen. "*Mademoiselle* Camille," she said to me, "I've sent for the remedies that the doctor prescribed. But he shall not come back; I would not hear of it."

What did such an injunction mean on her part? Did she know something, and was she afraid to know more? That is what I wondered to myself, without replying to her remarks in any way. When we were in bed, Sara told me that the doctor had had a long discussion with her mother. But that was all. It was enough to fill me with fears, which my friend shared with me! ! ! On that occasion, as I since learned, this man, without explaining himself openly to her, had asked Madame P. a host of very delicate questions about me, which she had hardly answered, being unable to give credence to the thought that motivated them. Suspicion could not enter into her soul; it would have been terrible; she energetically rejected it. Confronted by such blind obstinacy, the doctor did not think that he was obliged to take the initiative that his title and his faith as an honest man demanded of him; he was content to urge her to send me away from her house as quickly as possible, believing that he thus released himself from all responsibility.

I repeat: his duty traced out another line of conduct for him. In such a circumstance, indecision was not permitted; it was a grave fault, not only morally but in the eyes of the law. Terrified by the secret that he had come upon unexpectedly, he preferred to bury it forever!

Less informed than he, Madame P. was more to be excused, perhaps, although she was not entirely beyond reproach. The matter was worth the trouble of being examined. Undoubtedly, another woman would not have shown the same weakness. Far from being angry with the doctor, she should have thanked him and sought some way to get out of the difficulty. She did not do so for several reasons, all of them bad.

First of all, she was afraid of a scandal that might harm the respectability of her house and compromise her interests. Then, she had boundless trust in me. To accept the insinuations of the doctor was to doubt her daughter at the same time, and her pride rebelled at that idea. She drove her naïveté so far as to believe that I was completely ignorant of my position . . . That was absurdity pushed to the last degree! ! ! I have never been able to understand how a woman of her age, of her experience, could preserve such an illusion! Shouldn't the affection that Sara showed me have opened her eyes? It did not. She was afraid that by showing us the slightest suspicion she would put us on our guard. Poor woman! ! !

This incident, grave though it was, did not in any respect change our ordinary way of living. Madame P. had recovered her serenity, we our gaiety. On our excursions outside, we often ran across Doctor T. I would nudge Sara with my elbow. As he passed, he would always greet me with a smile! What must he have thought when he saw us laughing, the pair of us! ! ! What a strange situation! . . . His silence, his attitude in my regard, seemed a revolting enormity to me!

Several times I had the idea of provoking an explanation on his part by calling his attention to the falsity of the situation, which I had to get out of, whatever the price might be. Sara absolutely rejected any decision of that kind. For her it was no longer a matter of making amends; she thought only of the shame, the slander that would be attached to her entire life. Alas! I understood!

After having stigmatized, as it were, an intimacy that was outwardly innocent, would people be indulgent toward a love affair? No, without any doubt; they would be pitiless! They would insist on making us bitterly expiate the silent happiness of two years! It had been bought dearly, that happiness!

My pursuits had not been interrupted. One day in Sara's presence Madame P. gave me motherly recommendations concerning my health. Without being sick, I was really fatigued, weak. My nights were disturbed.

An almost continual if not abundant sweat increased my indisposition even more. Every evening before bedtime a drink was prepared for me, which was kept warm all night by the flame of a nightlight. "You won't forget to take it, will you, *Mademoiselle* Camille?" Madame P. said to me.

"Don't worry, Mama," Sara said. "I'm sleeping with her. I'll attend to it."

Her mother bridled up all at once. "As for that, I positively forbid you to do it! I have my reasons. And I shall add that if my authority is not enough, I would have recourse to another's. I am making it a matter of conscience for you." We did not answer, and with good reason.

What a bizarre contradiction! This woman blushed to herself because of the intimacy of our relations, yet she tolerated my presence in an institution of that kind. She saw a danger for her daughter in a night spent at my side; she did not see any in our sharing the same room, in our living the same life, in that habitual exchange of familiar attentions, caresses, kisses! . . .

This all seemed very innocent to her, no doubt. Even now I am still looking for the key to that enigma. It escapes me.

At that moment we began a new phase of our existence, from which might spring a danger that we were no longer the only ones to dread. An active though dissembled watch was kept over every step we took. Despite her apparent tranquility, Madame P. had lost her studied indifference, from which the warnings of the doctor had been unable to arouse her. Once again she had strictly forbidden her daughter to share my bed. This was a belated compromise, which had become more dangerous than useful.

In fact, how could it be supposed that we would be able to respect this prohibition, solemn though it was? Wasn't Nature being asked to make a heroic sacrifice, of which she was incapable?

To ward off suspicion, we decided that in the evening we

would each go to bed separately. Only, in the middle of the night, the first one who woke up would go to stay with the other until the next morning. In this way, barring unforeseen events, nobody was able to catch us by surprise, since the dormitories were completely separated from the main part of the house, and Madame P. never went there.

In the course of the summer, I received the visit from the superintendent of the arrondissement. He was as I desired him to be, that is to say, courteous and benevolent. Ordinarily he was escorted by the curé. This time he came alone. I definitely did not please our worthy pastor. That, at least, had the merit of sparing me his presence, to which I did not exactly attach great value! . . .

A new baby was expected in the family. Sara's younger sister was going to be a mother for the first time. It is unnecessary to say that everybody was awaiting this moment with the keenest impatience! The young woman came to the house every day. The preparations were made.

As I was Sara's *intimate girlfriend*, nobody was constrained in my presence; naturally, I was initiated into all those secret little details that are exchanged among persons of the same sex! ! . . .

One night my friend and I had been sleeping for a short time when there was a knocking on the door of the stairway that opened onto the two rooms. The servant came to announce the birth of a little girl. Seized by labor pains just as she was going to bed, the young woman had taken her husband's arm and gone in great haste to her mother's house. Two or three hours afterward she gave birth to a daughter.

We immediately went downstairs, hardly dressed, driven by curiosity as much as by interest. Madame P. was beaming with joy. I approached the bed where the young woman was resting. She reached out her hands to both of us with an expression of ineffable rapture!

Suffering had beautified her features even more and had given them that particular charm that reveals all the joys of maternity. She pointed to the cradle, which was at her side. Sara uncovered the little creature and kissed her all over.

I contemplated this scene with an emotion that I had great difficulty containing! ! ! . . .

Standing between the two beds, I looked back and forth at Sara and the baby. I could not tear my eyes away from them! ! ! . . .

My emotion had not escaped Madame P. She was watching me attentively, not knowing how to explain the reverie in which I was plunged . . . If the bandage that covered her eyes had been less thick, if her blindness had been less great, no doubt the truth might have appeared to her in all its brilliance, and replaced her imperturbable trust with fright! ! ! Did she prefer to remain in doubt rather than approach that terrible mystery? That may be . . .

Every day I would spend long hours in that room. Madame G.'s condition was most satisfactory.

When she was able to get up, she would come to visit us during the recreation period, nursing her baby before our eyes! ! !

Sara idolized her little niece. She envied her sister because of her! Who knows! ! !

In the midst of the happiness that intoxicated me, I was frightfully tormented. What was I to do, my God, what was I to decide on?

My poor mind was a chaos in which I could distinguish nothing. Confide in my mother? But it was enough to kill her! No! I could not initiate her into such a discovery!

Prolong the situation indefinitely?

If I did so, I would inevitably expose myself to the greatest misfortunes! I would outrage the most inviolable, the most sacred moral principles!

And could I not be called to account later for my guilty silence, and burdened with the sorry consequences that others should have foreseen? . . .

The vacation period was approaching. Again I was going to part company with my dearly beloved Sara. Our good-byes were sad, mine above all, for I was not sure of seeing her again . . . I left her without telling her about my plans.

I arrived at B. with death in my soul.

They were going to demand explanations from me that I was resolved not to give. Monsieur de Saint-M. was constrained, embarrassed. All my letters had been read to him.

He sought in vain to discover what they meant. My sadness distressed him. Without understanding it, he foresaw some catastrophe. His fear was further increased by the painful silence into which I obstinately withdrew.

It was thus that my mother and he awaited my confession, which did not come. A month had passed by in that fashion. The moment of departure was approaching.

My strength was exhausted. I saw it coming with terror, that inevitable moment! . . . My mother was more courageous. I had only a few more days left to be with her!

One morning I saw her enter my room and sit down near my bed. "Camille," she said to me, "you've understood, haven't you, that you can't go away from us like this. Your inconceivable words and behavior call for an explanation, which I beg you to give me." She could say no more. Her voice was trembling. I bowed my head and for two or three minutes I did not answer her!

Suddenly, a flash of light crossed my mind. "Very well, then," I said. "You want to know, and you shall know everything. But not today! Wait until tomorrow. That's all I ask of you." She withdrew.

That night I did not sleep for a second. I was out of bed at four o'clock in the morning. I got dressed in the wink of an eye. Nobody was up in the house. I noiselessly opened all the doors and found myself in the street.

In the ordinary circumstances of life I have often lacked courage, initiative.

In the presence of danger I recover. Misfortune finds me full of strength. So it was at this moment, when the future of my whole life was at stake . . . The struggle that was likely to follow gave me a preternatural vigor.

At five o'clock I was kneeling in the chapel of the bishopric. Monseigneur de B. said mass every day at that hour. When the mass was over, he was to be found in the confessional. The eminent prelate had a worldwide reputation. A man of genius par excellence, the Bishop of Saintes enjoyed an incontestable supremacy in the French episcopate. As for the people of his diocese, they were exceptionally devoted to him. They were proud of him. I had understood that here alone would I find counsel and protection.

When the mass was finished, I beckoned to the valet who served him and requested that he notify His Excellency. He came back immediately and told me to go into the sacristy. I approached it not with fear but with an energy that sprang from despair.

I received the episcopal blessing, and I knelt down upon the prie-dieu reserved for penitents. My confession was complete. It must have been long. The prelate had listened to me with a religious astonishment. It was not in vain that I had counted upon his indulgence. My words were a cry of supreme distress to which his great soul was not indifferent; his penetrating look had measured the depth of the abyss that lay open beneath my feet . . . The total frankness of my avowals predisposed him in my favor.

Everything that the Christian religion can offer by way of encouragement, consolation—I felt it then! . . . The few moments that I spent in the presence of that very great man are perhaps the most beautiful ones of my life. "My poor child," he said to me when he had finished his questioning, "I don't yet know how all this is going to turn out. Will you authorize me to make use of your secrets? For, although I know what to think in regard to yourself, I cannot be a judge in such a matter. I shall see my doctor this very day. I will come to an understanding with him about what course of action to take. So, come back tomorrow morning, and be at peace."

I was at the bishopric the next morning at the same hour. Monseigneur was expecting me. "I've had an interview with Doctor H.," he said. "Go to his office today with your mother." I had informed her the day before. Her anxiety cannot be described. At the hour mentioned, we were at the doctor's. He was not what is called a widely known doctor; but he was a man of science in the full sense of the word.

He had understood all the gravity of the mission that had been entrusted to him. It flattered his pride, because certainly it was the first case of this kind that had come his way, and I must say that he was equal to it.

I had not, however, expected such a thorough examination on his part.

It displeased me to see him initiate himself into my dearest secrets, and I answered in not very restrained terms certain of his remarks that seemed to me to be a violation.

He said to me then, "Here you must regard me not only as a doctor but also as a confessor. I must not only see for myself, I must also know everything you can tell me. This is a grave moment for you, more so than you think, perhaps. I must be able to answer for you with complete assurance, before Monseigneur first of all, and also, no doubt, before the law, which will appeal to my evidence." I shall excuse myself from entering here into the minute details of this examination, after which science conceded that it was convinced.

It now remained for him to bring about the correction of an error that had been committed beyond the bounds of all the ordinary rules. To do so, it was necessary to instigate a judgment that would rectify my civil status.

"Frankly," the good doctor said to me, "your godmother had a stroke of luck when she called you Camille. Give me your hand, *mademoiselle*; before long, I hope, we shall call you differently. When I leave you, I will go to the bishopric. I don't know what Monseigneur will decide, but I doubt that he will permit you to return to L. There, your position is lost; it is not tolerable. What amazes me is that my colleague at L. compromised himself to the point of letting you stay there for so long, knowing what you are. As for Madame P., her naïveté cannot be explained." He then addressed a few encouraging remarks to my poor mother, whose stupefaction was at its height. "It's true that you've lost your daughter," he said to her, "but you've found a son whom you were not expecting."

Our entry into Monsieur de Saint-M.'s room was an event.

The noble old man was walking up and down in order to relieve his feverish impatience. Seeing us, he stopped; my mother led him to his armchair and sat down at his feet. I took a position some distance away, not very eager to begin the account of what had just happened. From time to time Monsieur de Saint-M. raised his eyes to me and responded with an exclamation to the details that my mother was giving him. He was stupefied at first, then confronted the situation more calmly, also calculating that it might give me a more advantageous position in the future. With the right kind of influences, that could be hoped for. "All the same," he said, "I had to reach the age of eighty in order to witness such a dénouement, and you, Camille, were the one who was to procure it for me! May you be happy later, poor child!" I was so disturbed that I could not answer; my delirious imagination could not fasten on a serious, carefully considered thought.

At moments I wondered if I were not the plaything of an impossible dream.

This inevitable outcome, which I had foreseen, had even desired, terrified me now like a revolting enormity. In short, I had provoked it, no doubt it was my duty to have done so; but who knows? Perhaps I had been wrong. Didn't this abrupt change, which was going to reveal me in such an unexpected way, offend all the laws of conventional behavior? . . .

Was it likely that society, which is so severe, so blind in its judgments, would give me credit for an impulse that might pass for honesty? Wouldn't people try to falsify it instead and treat it as if it were a crime on my part?

Alas! At the time I could not indulge in all of these considerations. The way was open; I was driven to it by the thought of the duty that had to be fulfilled. I did not calculate.

On the following day I went to the bishopric. Monseigneur was expecting me. "I have seen the doctor," he said to me, "and I know everything. After careful thought, this is what I have decided: you are going to return to L. for a few more days, so as to remove from your departure the scandal it might have, both for you and for the school that you direct. I am giving you here a great proof of my trust. Do not abuse it. Have yourself replaced as soon as possible and come back here, after which we shall think about the way to make a new place for you in society."

Two days later I was at L. Sara, informed that I was coming, was waiting for me. After our first kisses she was struck by the look of deep seriousness that showed on my face. As she remarked about it to me, I sat down on the edge of my bed, casting her a pained glance. "My beloved," I said to her in a moved tone of voice, "the hour of separation has come"; and I told her briefly about what had just taken place at B. I can still see her dear, sweet face and the somber look of sadness that distorted it. She did not speak, but her dull gaze seemed to reproach me for the important decision that I had taken without consulting her, as if it were a mistake. "If you had wished," said that gaze, "we could have been happy for many days longer. But no doubt I am not enough any more; you are thirsty for a free, independent existence, which I cannot give you."

In fact, there was all that in the kind of disgust that had seized hold of me. I was no longer living. The shame that I felt because of my present position would alone have sufficed to make me break with a past for which I blushed.

That vast desire for the unknown made me egotistic and prevented me from regretting the very dear ties that I was going to break of my own free will.

Later I was to repent bitterly what I then regarded as an imperative duty. Society was soon to teach me that I had shown stupid weakness, and was to punish me cruelly for it.

The few days that I spent at L. were truly painful. My poor Sara could not always conceal the tears that weighed heavily on her. She carefully avoided the presence of her mother, who herself—is it believable?—could not get used to the idea that I was leaving for good.

I had had the matter out with her, and though I had not gone into the details of the considerations behind my action, I had been forced, in order to make her feel the full gravity of them, to invoke the authority of Monseigneur de B., whose express will no longer left me any freedom of choice.

That blind mother responded to these vague motives, which should have been a terrible warning to her, with a real or feigned incredulity that goes beyond all belief. Nevertheless, I can explain it to myself. As long as I was under her roof, she could not give an obvious reason for my behavior without putting herself on a hostile footing with me. That would have awakened the suspicions of her family and people at large, something she wanted to avoid at any cost. At bottom, she commended me, I cannot doubt that, and her apparent confidence hid horrible anxieties of which her daughter was the object. For if she had shut her ears until then to the evidence, to the suggestions of her doctor, she was permitted to do so no longer. The truth was appearing to her in its full light, and what must have been her sorrow when she thought about the consequences of her culpable trust! However, there was nothing in her words, in her gestures, that betrayed the state of her soul. She was either a truly strong woman or a foolishly ignorant one. In the presence of Sara and her other children she played an admirable role—one of touching simplicity, without any affectation—that put her beyond the reach of the slightest criticism. Was her affection for me feigned? I do not know. In any case, the most prejudiced mind would have been taken in by it. We all deceived one another and we were deceived, and that with the best faith in the world.

Never did a stranger, a more difficult situation, bring three people together in a community of ideas that was all shameful duplicity, incredible playacting in which feelings were confessed with the most magnificent sang-froid.

For Madame P., I was and I was always to be her daughter's chosen companion.

Before her mother and the others, Sara missed me as a *girlfriend*, as a *sister* whose absence she could openly lament without anybody taking exception to her behavior. Some initiate to all these mysteries who might have seen the three of us together, talking about how many days I would go on staying in the house at L., might have believed that he was at a performance of *Figaro* or at the Théâtre du Gymnase, and it is certain that no idolized actor ever put more truth into an improbable role.

One afternoon, while the students were at recreation, I followed Sara into her room. My departure was always the subject of our conversation and the cause of fresh tears. My friend, who was standing at her window, a hand around my neck, was weeping silently, when her mother suddenly entered with her younger sister.

The two of them sat down naturally, as if to share in our sorrow. Madame P. gazed at us tranquilly. *"Mademoiselle Camille,"* she said to me, "don't you see how much we are going to miss you? Why do you persist in your determination to leave us? Who will replace you with Sara, with me?" I would be unable to describe the effect these words produced on me. I was confounded by them. It was the height of ingenuous audacity. It was tempting God.

Should I have answered with a brutal confession, thus withering that chaste flower whose perfume still intoxicated me? No, certainly not. Sara would rather have died than been caught blushing in the presence of her mother and her sister. The secret of our love would have to be kept between God and myself.

So I answered that a power beyond my own will obliged me to leave promptly, without looking back. The young woman who was present at this conversation kept silent, and I understood instinctively that my secret was no longer unknown to her.

Sara took up all of her attention; she carefully watched every one of her movements. The poor child, who had given herself up completely to her grief, did not see that. She went on holding me in her embrace. Her tears were accompanied by expressive sobs. The hour for class put an end to this scene, during which I was in agony.

A few days later Madame P. went away. Upon her return, she informed me that she had managed to have me replaced, thanks to the superintendent of the arrondissement. And so, with great anguish of heart, I got ready to leave at any moment. The girl who had been announced at length arrived; I recognized her as a former student of the normal school of D. Our relations were rather cold. Her presence was a perpetual embarrassment for me, and the sign that separation was henceforth inevitable.

Witnessing the intimacy that bound me to Sara and her mother's regrets, she tried in vain to discover the reasons for my abrupt departure. She was soon convinced that, following the example of my aunt, who had been her classmate, I was going to become a nun. Her supposition made me smile. But I did not think it necessary to disabuse her of her notions.

I was to remain two or three days more in order to acquaint her with our method of teaching, not that I considered it necessary but because Madame P. had asked me to do so.

Sara did not speak to her very much. She had disliked her immediately. It had to be that way! The girl might take my place, but she could not replace me.

The very evening of her arrival, I revealed my intention to give her my bed in the dormitory, which was now to be her own, and to occupy Sara's little room in the main part of the building. My friend tried to dissuade me from doing so; her mother commended me. So, we were separated that first night; but the next day Sara came to bid me her daily good morning, then washed and dressed with me. It went on that way until my departure, which was irrevocably set for the end of the week.

The curé had been informed of it in a letter from Monseigneur de B., now the Archbishop of . . . So, out of sheer courtesy, I went to speak to him about it. I bitterly regretted having gone. That absurd man did not find an encouraging word to say to me about the incredible situation that had befallen me. Nothing could bend the inflexible rigor of that man. He never forgave me. What had I done to him? Nothing. Needless to say, I did not return to bid him good-bye, although Madame P. had asked me to do so.

I saw no one at L., and although they already knew about my departure, it took place without causing a stir, if not without the inevitable unkind remarks that feed the gossip of provincial busybodies.

My final day had come. I was at last going to leave this quiet retreat, the witness of my hidden joys. I was going to see, from a new perspective, a world I had never imagined.

My inexperience prepared me only for sadness and disillusionment. I saw everything then in a light that was radiant and free of clouds. Poor fool that I was! I possessed happiness, true felicity, and with gaiety of heart I was going to sacrifice all that—for what? For an idea, a stupid fear! ! ! Oh! I have thoroughly atoned for my folly! ! But what is the use of laments, regrets? I submitted to my destiny, I fulfilled—courageously, I believe—the painful duties of my situation. Many people will laugh. I pardon them, and I hope they shall never know the nameless sorrows that have overwhelmed me! ! !

My preparations were finished. I had said my last good-byes to my students. Poor, dear girls! With what emotion I had kissed their young brows! I had contemplated them lovingly, reproaching myself, almost, for the days that I had spent with them in such great, in such close intimacy!

It was seven o'clock in the morning. Sara was to accompany me as far as the highway, where the carriage passed by. I was frightfully sad at heart when I approached Madame P. to take leave. She, for her own part, was suffering violently. The pained contraction of her features said as much. There were many things in her silence. Regret, first of all; for, in spite of everything, she cared for me, sincerely, loyally. But along with this spontaneous affection there was resentment, I no longer doubt that. She saw everything clearly then.

Could she pardon me for the mysterious role that I had played in her house, with her daughter, whose purity was so dear to her? Still, I cannot believe that she suspected the *intimacy* of our relations. No, for she would have been struck down by the violence of her feelings. My good faith was a sure guarantee to her of the chastity of her child.

What uncommon and deplorable naïveté on the part of a mother! . . . In her ignorance of the facts of life, she could not admit that I might reappear in society with a name, a status, that were appropriate to my sex. "So, dear Camille," she said to me, "someday perhaps I shall have to call you *monsieur!* Oh, no! Tell me that won't happen!"

"That will happen, however, Madame, and in a little while, no doubt. Why don't you ask Monseigneur de B.?"

"But really, what will people say? The scandal that will result from this will inevitably fall on my house! And then!"

That was her greatest preoccupation, her nightmare. She saw her boarding school ruined, her reputation seriously hurt. Confronted by this prospect, she forgot her daughter; she did not think about what the past had been but about what the future would be.

"Now, good-bye, dear *daughter!*" And the excellent woman could say no more; Sara had turned away, holding back her tears. I beckoned to her and we left, taking a roundabout road in order to avoid going through the town. I had taken her arm, and I hugged it tight against my breast. She, from time to time, gave me a squeeze of her hand. Our looks met then and eloquently made up for the sentences that died upon our lips.

What man, seeing us clasped together like that, could have discovered the mysterious drama of those two young lives that outwardly were so calm, so gentle?

Doesn't the truth sometimes go beyond all imaginary conceptions, however exaggerated they may be? Have the *Metamorphoses* of Ovid gone further?

I clasped her for one last time in my arms, the girl whom I called my sister and whom I loved ardently, with all the passion of my twenty years. My lips brushed her own. Everything had been said between us. This time as I left I was bearing away in my soul all the happiness that I had enjoyed during those years, the first, the unique love of my life. As the carriage moved off, my beloved faded out of sight. It was all over.

I believe that I have said everything concerning this phase of my existence as a *girl*. They were the fine days of a life that was henceforth doomed to abandonment, to cold isolation. O my God! What a fate was mine! But You willed it, no doubt, and I shall say no more. Back again at B., I had to attend to the proceedings that related to my appearing in society as a member of the masculine sex.

Doctor H. had already prepared a voluminous report, a masterpiece in the medical style, intended to ensure before the courts a petition for rectification, which was to be ordained by the court of L., my birthplace. Armed with this document, I set out for that town; I was also provided with special recommendations for the presiding judge and the imperial attorney. My mother accompanied me. Our first visit was to the old curé, who had known my family for a long time. I shall not attempt to give here an idea of his naïve astonishment when he read the letter that Monseigneur de B. had written to him on this subject. It will be easily understood. Such cases are rare enough to excite curiosity. Monsieur de V., the presiding judge of L., gave us a warm welcome. When he had acquainted himself with the facts and asked me a few questions, he said to us, "You are going to go on my behalf to Monsieur D., my lawyer, and give him all these documents. The rest will be done without you. If your presence should be necessary later, you will be advised." We left the very next day, without having informed my family about what was being prepared for me. I wanted to keep it a secret until the dénouement, which was forthcoming. An exception was made for a single person: my maternal grandfather. He was terrified, for he wrongly foresaw an outcome that would be dangerous to the peace of all of us. I calmed him as best I could, assuring him that everything would take place legally and properly.

So, nobody besides himself knew the motive for our journey; however, I must report certain remarks, strange to say the least, that were made about myself and that were all confided to me afterward. An intimate woman friend of my mother's had been especially struck by my bearing, by my appearance, by my manner, which was just a bit cavalier.

It was the same elsewhere, at the hospital where I had stayed for three years—that is to say, until I was ten years old—among the young orphan girls of my age. With infinite pleasure, I had seen the chaplain there again. The good Mother Superior still called me her *dear daughter*. She accompanied us to the door, chatting. During that time, one of the girls of the house, of whom I had been the favorite companion, observed us from a window. Cleverly, she remarked that I was holding my umbrella under my left arm and that I had my right hand, which was ungloved, behind my back. That appeared to her to be rather graceless on the part of a *schoolmistress*. Moreover, my way of moving was in keeping with my face, with its hard and severely pronounced features.

I had been back at B. for almost two weeks when the lawyer who was charged with the petition informed me that the court, in a first audience, had named Doctor G. to undertake a new examination before it made a final judgment, and that my presence at the doctor's was necessary.

I had to resign myself. Besides, that was what I was expecting.

Needless to say, the second examination had the same result as the first, and in conformity with the report to which it led, the civil court of L. ordained that a rectification be made on the civil status registers, which meant that I was to be entered there as belonging to the masculine sex, and at the same time I was to be given a new first name in place of the feminine one I had received when I was born.

I was at B. when this decree was handed down. They sent me the record of the judgment, which was later registered in the *Annales de médecine légale.*

Consulting this work, I discovered that a similar case had occurred in 1813, in a department in the Midi, if not under the same circumstances, at least with the same outcome.

So, it was all over. According to my civil status, I was henceforth to belong to that half of the human race which is called the stronger sex. I, who had been raised until the age of twenty-one in religious houses, among shy female companions, was going to leave that whole delightful past far behind me, like Achilles, and enter the lists, armed with my weakness alone and my deep inexperience of men and things.

Dissembling was no longer to be thought of. People were already talking in whispers. The little town of L. was aroused by this extraordinary event, which by its nature excited criticism and slander. As always, the matter was considerably embroidered upon. Some people went so far as to accuse my mother of having concealed my true sex in order to save me from conscription. Others saw me as a real Don Juan, saying that I had brought shame and dishonor everywhere, and had profited brazenly from my situation in order to engage secretly in love affairs with women who had been consecrated to the Lord. I knew all that, and I was not in any way upset by it.

At B. it was a very different thing. I was seen attending mass one fine morning dressed as a man, in the company of Madame de R., the daughter of Monsieur de Saint-M. Only one or two people had recognized me; that was quite enough. Soon, the whole town was talking about it.

The newspapers joined in. The next day all of them reported the event. One of them modestly compared me to Achilles spinning at the feet of Omphale; but among these flowers of rhetoric were mingled insinuations that were treacherous both to myself and to others. After the departmental press came the more or less piquant articles by some editors whose names I have not forgotten; these were reproduced immediately by certain Paris newspapers. The high society of the town was excited by them. I was the subject of all the conversations at the seashore bathing establishment. Some persons of standing were there that day with the prefect, who proclaimed his astonishment loudly. Fortunately for me, I was protected by the name of Monseigneur de B. They knew about the part that the eminent prelate had played in the affair, and so they were forced to yield. The very next day I went to pay him a visit in my new dress, which allowed him then to show me more freely all the affectionate benevolence that he had for me. His Excellency clasped my hand warmly, calling me his friend! The memory of this scene is still vivid in my mind.

I shall never forget everything I owe that man, who lived the Gospel and was truly worthy of his high position, as much through the loftiness of his rare genius as through the immense generosity of his soul. I had also seen Doctor H. "If you'll take my advice," he said, "you'll go along with me to the prefecture. The prefect wants to see you, and I don't doubt that he will be disposed to help you. He can do everything for you, especially at this time."

So there I was with the doctor in the office of the prefect, to whom my visit seemed to give pleasure. He received me like a father and questioned me in a friendly fashion about my past and about my plans for the future. My position was difficult, it interested him. I do not very well know why the idea of joining the railroad had occurred to me. I spoke about it to the prefect, who did not disapprove of it. He promised me that he would submit a request to the company of . . . Then, smiling gaily, he said to me, "You know what a storm you've raised and the many misdeeds that you are accused of. Don't pay any attention to all that. Walk with your head up; you have the right to do so. It will be difficult for you, perhaps. That's understandable. Also, and this is a good piece of advice that I'm giving you, resign yourself to leaving this region for a while. I'm going to look after that." I appreciated the rightness of this advice better than anybody. I felt the need for a temporary absence, and I deeply desired it.

As I had feared, hateful rumors circulated among the public concerning the intimacy of my relations with Mademoiselle Sara. According to some, she was really dishonored. Oh! I confess it, I felt that blow most of all. It was insupportable to me, the idea of seeing that poor child become the victim of the fatality that was overwhelming me. Society, that pitiless judge, could sully with impunity the holy affection of two loyal souls who had been cast together upon the edge of a secret abyss and whose inevitable fall had been the mysterious bond between them. Stupid blindness of the crowd, which condemns when it should absolve!

I knew her well enough to be perfectly convinced that she would suffer courageously and in silence, without condemning me on that account. She alone understood me, perhaps. She alone loved me! For a very long time her adored memory sustained me, gave me the strength to live! ! Even today, when everything seems to have forsaken me and when frightful solitude has grown around me, as if my unhappiness were fatal to everything that touches me, I feel a certain sweet joy thinking that there is a being in this world who deigned to share in my miserable existence and who keeps a little tender pity for the poor forlorn creature that I am. Is that only an illusion, perhaps? Perhaps at the moment I am writing these lines she has forever banished from her heart the one for whom she was the unique happiness. My God! What remains to me then? Nothing. Cold solitude, dark isolation! Oh! To live alone, always alone, in the midst of the crowd that surrounds me, without a word of love ever coming to gladden my soul, without a friendly hand reaching out to me! What a terrible, nameless punishment! Who will ever be able to understand it? To carry in oneself ineffable treasures of love and to be condemned to hide them like a shameful thing, like a crime! To have a soul of fire and to say to oneself: Never shall a virgin grant you the sacred rights of a husband. That supreme consolation of men here below—I am not to enjoy it. Oh, death! Death will truly be the hour of deliverance for me! Another wandering Jew, I await it as the end of the most frightful of all torments! ! ! But You remain to me, my God! You have willed that I belong to no one here below, through none of those earthly bonds that elevate man by perpetuating Your divine work! Though I am a sad disinherited creature, I can still lift up my eyes to You, for You at least will not reject me!

Five or six weeks after my visit to the prefect, I received the invitation to go to Paris, to present myself to the head of operations of the railroad of . . . This letter filled me with joy. To the prospect of a journey to Paris was added the hope of promptly leaving a region that I had come to abhor, and of finally escaping from that kind of ridiculous inquisition of which I saw myself the object. The prefect, whom I went to see at once, sincerely shared my satisfaction and urged me not to delay my departure. My poor mother was radiant, although the idea of a forthcoming separation mingled sadness with the joy she felt because of this compensation, which already appeared to her as the dawn of a shining future.

Always good and farsighted, Monsieur de Saint-M. earnestly recommended me to one of his grandnephews in Paris, where he had been living for a long time. He was not a stranger to me. He knew me. He knew my mother and was aware of the real attachment that his whole family had devoted to her. And so he gave me a brother's welcome. Thanks to him, I was spared the terrible confusion that provincials experience when they are thrown for the first time, and alone, into the whirlpool of Paris, that tumultuous city.

The day after my arrival he accompanied me to the administrative offices of . . . , where I saw the head of operations, Monsieur . . . , whose name I shall not divulge here, as it is too well known. In the short interview I had with him, I asked to be called to Paris as a favor, which he promised me. These were his final words: "Return to B. and await your nomination at the earliest possible time."

So I left Paris two days later, having barely caught a glimpse of it but counting very much on seeing it again more fully. The time that I spent at B. was not disturbed by any serious incident. I went out every day and always alone. The stir caused by my adventure was beginning to die down. The situation was better appreciated now that it stood out in broad daylight. I must say besides that the people who knew me very well had shown me more sympathy since the scandal caused by the latest events. "Poor child," said a mother whose daughter had been my friend and classmate, "I like him better now, for I can appreciate him twice as well. He must really have suffered!"

I leave you to imagine the consternation of my excellent teachers in the normal school. It would be impossible to have any idea of it. The venerable chaplain wrote me a very fatherly and friendly letter on this subject. "I can now, my dear son, tell you what true affection I have kept for my former *daughter*. But what you would be unable to understand is the naïve astonishment of our good nuns, of whom you were the favorite student, in a way. When I gave her the news about your transformation, Sister Marie-des-Anges covered her face with her hands, thinking of the close intimacy that once bound you to her. 'My God!' cried the chaste creature. 'I kissed him so heartily when he was staying here recently for the retreat, which I had invited him to attend!

And when he left me he kissed my hands without any scruple.'" But those good souls did not accuse me on that account, and their affection, although changing form, remained basically the same. That, I know, will not fail me, for it rests upon the purest, the most holy foundations.

Which is to say that all the suppositions that were made about my earlier relations with those angels on earth are false, completely false. No doubt they were permitted up to a certain point, and I cannot deny that I was terribly exposed, as is understandable; but I alone knew the danger. If I suffered, if I struggled, at least nobody suspected it. It is certainly owing to the solidity of the principles of my youth, to their extreme purity, that I did not have to blush in the presence of those pure brows, whose sweet serenity I left untroubled.

I have made these few remarks not to justify myself but because I would consider it a crime, a glaring piece of treachery, and would reproach myself accordingly, if by my silence I fostered suspicions about creatures whose souls are above all else worthy of the attention of God.

My correspondence with Sara had not ceased. She received my letters, and she answered me regularly, though without her mother's knowledge. I no longer dared write to the latter. I was wrong not to, however, as I later understood. My fearful silence in her regard must have seemed to her to be either a sign of cold indifference to her or a belated admission that I had behaved guiltily in her house.

Here again my inexperience was my undoing. I cannot doubt that if I had known how to manage the situation my future would have been different. Today, perhaps, I would be her son-in-law.

But God no doubt did not will it to be, and I was wrong

to aspire to this title, which shall never be mine! Madame P. cared for me, her affection was motherly and sincere. My departure had hurt her in two ways, by threatening her in her dearest interests—the reputation of her daughter, which had been gravely compromised, and the good name of her house. Both of them were impaired, inevitably. People were whispering all around her. The present explained the past, which was already so equivocal. The superintendents of the Academy could not restrain themselves from broaching this very delicate subject with her. They knew about all the vicissitudes of this drama, in which the role that I had played stood out in a blazing light for everybody to see. To remind her of it in any way at all was to put her through all the torments of shame and fright, it was to cast doubt upon the respectability of her sensitively proud character. Under such circumstances, the poor woman must many times have cursed the day when she had taken me into her home. Her motherly heart must have been crushed by the terrible thoughts that came into her mind, and perhaps by the reproaches that were heaped upon her by her conscience, which had been blind for so long because she was loyal, and because suspecting her child was beneath her. Still, my God! She was a woman, and as such she could know the limits of human strength!

A month after I had left Paris I received the order to return there and place myself at the disposal of the head of operations of the railroad of . . . I left; but first I went to pay a final visit to Monseigneur. The thought that I was no doubt leaving him for a very long time was painful to me. It is so rare that one meets such men who combine all the qualities of the soul with the wealth of a great mind. His Excellency had been very deeply touched by the exceptional situation in which he had met me. He had become attached to me, if I may say so. The good prelate took my hand; then, hugging me warmly against his heart, he blessed me. I was overcome. I could only bow my head in silence, then stammer a few words of thanks as I withdrew.

My poor mother shed tears when we separated, and in spite of all my efforts I must confess that I imitated her. In twenty-four hours we were going to be five hundred miles apart from each other, and for the first time. We surely had the right to a few regretful tears. It is true that we had hopes of seeing each other again. That was not the case for my noble and revered benefactor, Monsieur de Saint-M. On the verge of death, he could no longer hope. "My poor Camille," he said to me with sobs in his voice, "we shall never meet again!" He clasped my hand with his own. I felt it trembling.

I know nothing more heartrending than an old man in tears. Oh! I felt my strength failing me in the presence of this grief, which bore witness to the deepest, the strongest affection. In fact, I felt a father's heart beating there. I knew it, and how proud I was!

Venerable man, rest in peace in your tomb! ! Death for you was the limit of an existence that was full of good works, of generous gifts for which your great soul has received its reward! May you hear my feeble voice! It will tell you that here below there is a heart full of the memory of you.

Now he is no more! This death broke in me a bond that nothing in the world could replace! ! ! I was deprived of being present at his final moments. He felt them approaching. He had an attack, a terrible attack. Still, he was able to pronounce the names of everything that he loved and to say good-bye to my mother. Joining her hands to his daughter's, he gazed at them both and died while pronouncing my name!

Two years have passed since that day. But I see him again still, whole in my heart. My devotion to him is the last, the unique joy of my life! Ah, how often since then, in the midst of the disgust, the bitterness that overwhelm me, I have caught glimpses of the frightful void hollowed out by his absence!

And now, alone! . . . alone . . . forever! Forsaken, outlawed in the midst of my brothers! Ah! What am I saying! Have I the right to give that name to those who surround me? No, I do not. I am alone! My arrival in Paris marks the beginning of a new phase of my double and bizarre existence. Brought up for twenty years among girls, I was at first and for two years at the most a *lady's maid*. When I was sixteen and a half I entered the normal school of . . . as a student-teacher. When I was nineteen I obtained my teaching certificate. A few months later I was directing a rather well-known boarding school in the arrondissement of . . . I left it when I was twenty-one. That was in the month of April. At the end of the same year I was in Paris, with the railroad of . . .*

Go, accursed one, pursue your fate! The world that you invoke was not made for you. You were not made for it. In this vast universe, where every grief has its place, you shall

---

* At this point the continuous reproduction of the manuscript is interrupted. The pages that follow are only extracts from the texts that Auguste Tardieu had in his possession. (M. F.)

search in vain for a corner where you may shelter your own, for it would be a blemish there. It overturns all the laws of nature and humanity. The family's hearth is shut to you. Your very life is a scandal for which the young virgin, the timid adolescent youth, would blush!

Among those degraded women who have smiled at me, whose lips have brushed my own, there is doubtlessly not one of them who would not have shrunk back in shame under the pressure of my embraces, as from the touch of a reptile. Ah, well! I shall not curse anyone, not I. Yes, I have passed by in your midst without leaving the shadow of a breath. Men! I have not soiled my lips with your false oaths, nor my body with your hideous copulations. I have not seen my name dragged in the mud by a faithless wife. I have been spared all the filthy sores that you display in broad daylight.

I have breathed in only the fragrance of that golden cup. You have drunk to the dregs all its shame, all its dishonor, still without being satisfied. So keep your pity to yourself.

You are to be pitied more than I, perhaps. I soar above all your innumerable miseries, partaking of the nature of the angels; for, as you have said, my place is not in your narrow sphere. You have the earth, I have boundless space. Enchained here below by the thousand bonds of your gross, material senses, your spirits cannot plunge into that limpid Ocean of the infinite, where, lost for a day upon your arid shores, my soul drinks deep.

Set free before its time from its virginal envelope, it has glimpsed with beatitude the luminous brightness of an immortal, resplendent world, its future and longed-for abode. Oh! Who could describe the surges of pure ecstasy of my soul, whose earthly ties to humanity have been broken. And from what a height it contemplates that closed horizon swarming with so much passion, so much hateful anger, so much materialism! And it is upon *me* that you will cast your insulting disdain, as upon a disinherited creature, a being without a name!

And you have the right to do so? You, degraded men, debased a thousand times over and forever useless, despicable and despised playthings of corrupted creatures, those women whom you flaunt like conquests. Do you, I say, cast sarcasm and outrage in my face? Ah, yes, be proud of your rights.

The slime that covers you is witness enough to the noble use that you have made of them. It is I, rather, who should be sorry for you, poor fallen spirits, who have exhausted all the living springs of your hearts in wretched satisfactions, who have extinguished down to the final ray of your intelligence that pure torch that was intended to guide your steps along the paths of life. Yes, I am sorry for you, for you have not suffered. You have lacked the noble, the great heart, the generous soul, that are needed in order to suffer. But the hour of expiation shall come, if it has not already come. And then you will be terrified by the frightful emptiness of your entire being.

Unfortunate men! You shall find nothing to fill it. You are coming to the threshold of eternity to regret—what? Life. In the presence of immortality you shall regret the dust, the nothingness!

I tell you this, I, whom you have trod beneath your feet—that I dominate you with the full height of my immaterial, virginal nature, with my long sufferings.

I say my long sufferings, and what I say is the truth, for I too have dreamed of those ecstatic nights, those burning passions, that were to be revealed to me only through intuition.

I shuddered like a tiger when, in the evening, under the blaze of chandeliers, I saw pass by those women who are beautiful because of their adornment rather than because of their long-since faded charms. Sitting sadly in the parterre of a theater, letting my bleak gaze wander over the whole circular enclosure, I secretly analyzed all the joys that were contained in those words dissembled behind fans, in those smiles that promised happiness with the pressure of a hand. Ah! Do not believe it! Do not believe I was not jealous under the shock of all those electric currents flowing from all directions, meeting and passing on. No. I was young. I too desired a place at that feast of love. And I was to belong to nobody—except to God. Before I arrived at that absolute detachment of a soul defeated by its very struggle, oh! believe it, I suffered cruelly!

In the midst of my ills I fostered a mad illusion, a guilty one, no doubt. But who would dare reproach me for it? A girl had loved me, as one loves for the first time. So she believed, at least.

In her innocent ignorance, she had dreamed of nothing beyond the incomplete joys that I revealed to her. Later, I was crushed by her forgetting me. That also brought me back to the truth of the situation, which I had forgotten for a moment.

It was then, after this last, this unique, happiness had been torn away from me that I really understood the extent of my duties and the painful sacrifice they demanded of me.

Immediately, unselfishly, I broke with all the memories of my past. I buried myself alive, young, in that eternal solitude that I find everywhere, in the midst of the turmoil of the crowds as much as in the most unfrequented retreat!

My reason, which had gone astray, was restored to me. With it I soon found oblivion again, if not peace or happiness.

Alas! Happiness has never been my lot.

Many days have passed since then. The break has been complete. Only in thought do I still converse with that dear shadow of an extinct love. I sometimes look back upon those days that have so quickly fled, those days of holy tenderness, of chaste illusions, when, a young man among girls, my sisters, my companions, I found that their sweet and intimate company was enough for my life, which not a breath had tarnished.

Such memories have nothing about them that is bitter. They are consolation for the many disappointments. They are a fragrant oasis in which my soul, wounded by stormy struggles, takes refuge. Today I confront the dark prospect of my implacable destiny with a calm mind.

Profoundly disgusted with everything and everyone, I endure the injustices of human beings, their hypocritical hatreds, without being disturbed by them. I have shut myself up in a retrenchment that is proof against their attacks.

There is an abyss between them and myself, a barrier that cannot be crossed . . . I defy them all.

May 30, 186 . . . —Lord! Lord! The cup of my sorrows, is it not yet empty, then? Must Your divine hand, then, spread out over me only to strike, only to break, this so profoundly embittered heart, so that no more room may be found in it either for joy or for hatred? Can my isolation be more complete? Can my abandonment be more painful?

Oh! pity, my God! Pity, for I am succumbing to that slow and frightful agony of death, for my strength is forsaking me, for the drop of water has become an ocean. It has invaded all the powers of my being.

It has hollowed out beneath my steps an ever vaster, an ever deeper, abyss into which I cannot look without feeling a horrible dizziness. It seems to me at times that this treacherous ground is going to cave in beneath my feet and swallow me up forever!

This incessant struggle of nature against reason exhausts me more and more each day, and drags me with great strides toward the tomb.

It is no longer years that remain to me but months, days perhaps.

I feel that in an obvious, terrible way, and how sweet, how consoling this thought is for my soul. Death is there, oblivion. There, without any doubt, the poor wretch, exiled from the world, shall at last find a homeland, brothers, friends. And there, too, shall the outlaw find a place.

When that day comes a few doctors will make a little stir around my corpse; they will shatter all the extinct mechanisms of its impulses, will draw new information from it, will analyze all the mysterious sufferings that were heaped up on a single human being. O princes of science, enlightened chemists, whose names resound throughout the world, analyze then, if that is possible, all the sorrows that have burned, devoured this heart down to its last fibers; all the scalding tears that have drowned it, squeezed it dry in their savage grasp!

Discover how many wounds scathing contempt, abuse, vile mockery, bitter sarcasm, have inflicted upon it, and you will have discovered the secret that the tombstone pitilessly keeps!....

Then they shall give a thought to the poor wretch whom, during his life, they shamefully rejected, blushing sometimes when they clasped his hand, to whom they even refused bread and the very right to live!

For I have come to that point. Reality is crushing me, is pursuing me. What is going to become of me? I do not know. Where can I find for tomorrow the bit of bread that is given by work?

Will I have to beg for it then, commit a crime for it? Having returned to this Paris that I like because I am ignored here, will I have to lie in wait some evening for a fortunate man to pass by, who will do me the favor of insulting me, while pointing me out to a policeman? And yet there is no door that I have not knocked on.

Allowed to see some prominent people who knew me, I asked, I begged them to come to my assistance. It would have been easy indeed for them to have done so. With their influence in Paris, they could with a word have given me a means of honorably earning my livelihood.

Oh! I must say it, I received warm protestations of devotion everywhere, which I was stupid enough to count on. That was a piece of sheer folly, from which I recovered very quickly. I finally understood that henceforth I had to count on myself alone. My feeble resources were exhausted. I would soon be forced to experience the pangs of destitution, the torments of hunger. For I had spent a month like that— asking, waiting, and always receiving negative responses to my overtures.

A final course of action remained to me; I adopted it, believing that this time I had found safety.

I resolutely went to enroll myself as a valet in one of those numerous refuges with which Paris swarms, in a placement office for servants. "Have you ever been a servant?" That was the question they asked me straight off.

And when I answered negatively: "You'll have difficulty finding something; but come back anyhow, and we'll see."

Alas! I went back every day, and every day I heard the same crushing answer.

I am not unaware that I am the object of extraordinary astonishment to everybody around me.

All those young faces that radiate the joy of their age seem to read upon my own face some frightful truth whose secret escapes them.

The cold fixity of my gaze seems to freeze them and forces them to be almost respectful.

How shall I define their strange attitude in my presence? I could not do so. But for me it is obvious, incontestable.

They themselves give in to it; they do not explain it.

Those carefree children of the Left Bank, those future masters of knowledge, who prepare for their successes between a kiss and a demitasse, with whom I am in daily contact, though only in restaurants, hardly explain to themselves, either, the kind of bleak savagery of my habits, which in fact cannot be explained in someone who is twenty-eight years old. Though I smile sometimes at the nice girls at the neighboring tables, not one of them in any case could say what pretty little face shares my poor room with me. And that is a bit of information that they can give with certainty about such or such a male student of the quarter, for all the girls know one another, even if they do not always like one another. They are perfectly up-to-date about the changes that go on continually in their reciprocal households, and about the exchanges that take place among their admirers of the night before and those of the day after.

There is really an interesting study to be made about these local customs. Without being involved in any intrigue, without being an actor in the comedy, I often witness strange scenes that occur between these loving couples. A simple spectator, I observe conscientiously, and I almost always conclude by telling myself that my role is best.

Looking down from the height of my proud independence, I establish myself as a judge. The real experience that I have acquired regarding the heart of a woman places me far above certain famous critics whose estimations, I must say, have struck me more than once by their falsity.

The younger Dumas, among others, has tried in vain to tear away that veil which can only be half-drawn aside, impenetrable as it is to the eyes of the profane.

"Thou shalt go no farther," he was answered.

In fact, he was arrested in his prodigious élan. Why? He lacked the password for penetrating into the sanctuary. He went astray in an interminable labyrinth, which he left exhausted, defeated, still not initiated into that knowledge he pretends to possess, that no man will ever possess.

Should we deplore that this must be so? No. Oh! no.

I shall say for my own part, and I am morally convinced of it, that not only is this knowledge impossible but it is absolutely necessary that it be so; there is a limit beyond which it would be dangerous for a man to go. His mental powers do not allow it, his happiness depends on his stopping short.

As the result of an exceptional situation, on which I do not pride myself, I, who am called a man, have been granted the intimate, deep understanding of all the facets, all the secrets, of a woman's character. I can read her heart like an open book. I could count every beat of it. In a word, I have the secret of her strength and the measure of her weakness, and so I would make a detestable husband for that reason. I also feel that all my joys would be poisoned in marriage and that I would cruelly abuse, perhaps, the immense advantage that would be mine, an advantage that would turn against me.

After many dealings at the placement office, they decided to give me a letter of introduction to a lady who was looking for a valet.

The Countess de J. lived in a little townhouse in the Faubourg Saint-Honoré.

I found her alone in a vast salon where she was writing. She took my letter, sat down in front of her fire, and asked me several questions, which I had been expecting. I had never been a servant, that was always the insurmountable obstacle.

I could very well have said to her, "I have been a *lady's maid*." But how could I answer with such an outrageous remark?

However, she passed over this important point.

"Here," the lady said good-naturedly, "you could learn your duties in a short time; but you look weak, delicate to me, and not at all cut out for work of that sort. So I cannot take you on here."

I was sent away.

Unfortunately, she was telling the truth.

I am weak and have a sickly appearance. In that condition, one finds hardly any place to stay, except at the hospital. That is where I shall end up, no doubt.

From time to time I went to visit an elegant young woman whose husband manages a café in the Palais-Royal.

My relations with her were very friendly. She knew my family a little, and the principal events of my life had excited her feminine curiosity to the highest pitch. And so, with the skill of her sex, she often found the means for leading the conversation onto that ground, always awaiting some mysterious confidence, with which I was never very lavish, even for her.

The impressions of my life are not such as can be thrown in all directions. They have to do with situations that few can appreciate, and it is certain that for some coarse people of our time there would be matter for a number of foolish interpretations of things and events, interpretations that would not always be without danger for me, as I have sometimes been in a position to judge.

I can give an example. At the railroad office an assistant manager was talking with me about the oddity of my past. He believed quite frankly that, sought after one day as a woman by a young man, I had yielded myself to his desires and that my real sex had then been discovered. You can see how far this capacity for judging me can go and what serious consequences it can have for me, for my peace of mind.

Admitted on a temporary basis into a financial administration, where I spent a few months in unclouded tranquility, it was possible for me to hope for permanent admission; but this did not come about. Changes occurred in the company, which obliged it to reduce its personnel. They thanked me, it is true, and allowed me to entertain the possibility of being reinstated in my position later on, but that could not be taken as a certainty.

So there I was, again looking for a livelihood. My resources could permit me to wait a month. Under these conditions I could believe that I was rich. I need so little. What I eat in a day would hardly be enough for the breakfast of a man of my age who was equipped with a good stomach.

As for anxiety, I can truly declare that I had none.

I consider that every day given to me is the last of my life. And I do so quite naturally, without the slightest dread.

To understand such indifference in someone who is twenty-nine, it would be necessary to have seen oneself condemned, like me, to the most bitter of all torments: perpetual isolation. The idea of death, which is generally so repulsive, is ineffably sweet to my aching soul.

The sight of a tomb reconciles me to life. It makes me feel an indefinable tenderness for the one whose bones are lying there beneath my feet. That man who was a stranger to me becomes a brother. I converse with his soul, which has been freed from its earthly chains; a captive, I devoutly pray for the moment when I shall be allowed to join him.

The emotion overcomes me to such a point that I feel my heart swelling with joy, with hope. I would weep, but very sweet tears.

I have felt very often what I am describing here, for my favorite walks in Paris are the ones I take in the Père-Lachaise, in the Montmartre cemeteries. Devotion to the dead has been born in me.

My temporary situation, unfortunately, threatened to last

too long. The wasting away of my finances made me susceptible to depressing thoughts.

Even with the prospect of being called back to work again, I could hardly allow this situation to continue, for I had come to the point of wondering how I would be able to have breakfast the next day.

May you, my readers, never know all the horror that is contained in this remark.

Such a situation, by being prolonged, can lead the wretch whom it overwhelms to the most frightful extremities. On that day I finally came to understand suicides and to excuse them.

This has no need of commentaries.

How many times, sitting sadly on a bench in the Tuileries, I yielded bit by bit to the attraction of despair, descending that terribly swift slope to depths from which—alas!—one can only return terror-stricken, heavy-hearted, and morally defeated.

Oh! How I craved the sleep of the tomb then, that final refuge of human nature. Why, then, Lord, have You prolonged until now an existence that is useless to everybody and so crushing for myself? That is one of the mysteries which it is not for man to fathom.

A burden to others and to myself, without any affection, without any of those prospects that at least sometimes brighten with their pure and tender rays the careworn brows of those who suffer. But no, nothing. Always abandonment, solitude, outrageous scorn.

A few days before, driven to the end of my endurance, I had to turn for help to my poor, good mother.

Let it be clearly understood how painful such a course

of action is on the part of a son who knows what privations this assistance will involve.

So not only did I see myself powerless to bring more happiness to the final days of the woman whom I owed so much, but I even had to lessen her resources, which were already so scanty.

I can very well declare that this is the most desperate extreme to which I could be condemned.

I am going to speak here about a disastrous resolution that the deep discouragement of those recent days prompted me to make. One morning in front of the Tuileries I came upon a man who I thought was still in the heart of Brittany, where I had known him some years before. He was the agent of an important shipping company.

I let him pass by without speaking to him, for he had not recognized me. Later, thinking about the strangeness of this encounter, I thought I saw in it an assurance of happiness for a new future.

The good memory that I had kept of our relations seemed to me like a guarantee of his good will toward me in my present situation.

On the day after the next, I went to pay him a visit at the central administrative offices of the company, and I did not hide from him any of the difficulties of my situation. He took an interest in it, I must admit. His welcome was even more affectionate than I had hoped it would be.

I asked him quite simply to let me sail on board a steamship as a waiter's assistant. My proposal astonished him a great deal.

He wished he could do better for me.

On the other hand, he pointed out to me the material

impossibilities that stood in the way of my carrying out my plan.

First of all, it was the company's policy to admit in this capacity only people who were already accustomed to sailing. "And then," he said, "I can't believe that you, with the kind of life you've led, are well suited to performing such a duty. If you absolutely insist on it, I am entirely disposed to help you. Perhaps, even, it will be possible for me to lighten your situation on board by recommending you to one of my friends, the purser on the *Europe*."

I accepted without hesitation. "Well, then," he said to me, "I shall see the director. But it would be good if you were to give me a recommendation for him, from a deputy, for example."

I went back the next day with a letter that I obtained without difficulty from a deputy of my department, Monsieur de V.

At this point, there was no backing down. I felt that very much. I had committed myself so quickly in order not to have to turn back any more.

All these steps had been taken, and I had still not consulted anybody, either my mother or my friends. I meant to inform them only at the moment of my departure, for they would certainly have dissuaded me from it if they had known in what status I was leaving. They never did know.

I was supposed to have a rather prompt answer, as the *Europe* had just arrived at Le Havre.

In the meantime, I received a notice to go that very day to the company of . . . , to resume my position there. This letter, which should have delighted me, struck me with consternation. I found myself in a strange predicament.

What was to be done? It was really very simple, and I had only one course of action to take: consult my excellent protector, admit to him frankly everything that I had done, and follow his advice. I did not do so.

With me, unfortunately, the first impulse is rarely the right one. Haste does not lead me to anything good. This circumstance is a new proof of that. I decided to remain silent and let events take their course.

As my departure for the United States could not take place for another month, nothing prevented me from temporarily reoccupying the position that had been offered to me. That is what I did, in fact.

The motive that had determined my recall was of a nature to make me hope I would be employed for a rather long time, and that is what they soon gave me to understand. And yet I spurned this prospect in order to attach myself even more to the foolhardy scheme I was waiting to see carried out.

A month passed by that way.

The closer my impending departure came, the more I felt secret anguish. I was so fortunate in the present. Why should I go and cast myself into a future that was uncertain at the least? Solely because I believed I had committed myself. A fine reason when serious interests are at stake.

To this fear was added the anxiety of having to abandon people who until then had been so good to me. That idea was bitter, painful to me. With a single word I might still have put an end to this cruel uneasiness, determinedly renouncing what I foolishly believed it was my duty not to refuse. This accursed obstinacy was a matter of false pride, which was surely very much misplaced. I did not want to weaken in my initial resolution. It is true that it had been made forcefully, but it had also been made under the influence of discouragement. The die had been cast. I submitted to my fate.

The purser of the *Europe* replied that he was going to take me on board his ship but simply as a waiter's assistant, since the regulations were opposed to my being employed, even at intervals, on the ship's records. This letter was cold, significant, and it plunged me again into indecision. Monsieur M. himself did not urge me to accept. He said he was saddened to see me leave on these terms, and at the same time he flattered me with the hope that my position might improve later, promising that he would do everything in his power to help me.

I braced myself against what I denounced as weakness, and with my heart heavy and full of misgiving, I tremblingly pronounced my final word of acceptance. That was on a Thursday. My departure was set for the following Monday.

I immediately wrote to my mother to announce it to her, while still being very careful not to let her know what position I was going to fill in the future. She would not have gotten over it.

The idea of this journey was already so painful for her that I could not go and aggravate the sadness of it with such a confession.

It will be understood that I kept the same reserve toward my protectors.

It was too late for others to advise me or reproach me. They let me go my own way, believing that I had been tempted by the lure of a favorable position. I let them keep this conviction, which up to a certain point might excuse my behavior.

What strange blindness was it that made me hold on to

this absurd role until the end? I would be unable to explain it to myself. Perhaps it was that thirst for the unknown, which is so natural to man.

. . . . .

In the month of February 1868, the corpse of Abel Barbin, who had committed suicide by means of a charcoal stove, was found in a room in the quarter of the Théâtre de l'Odéon. He had left the manuscript of the preceding text. (M. F.)

THE DOSSIER

I have been content to bring together some of the principal documents that concern Adélaïde Herculine Barbin. The question of strange destinies like her own, which have raised so many problems for medicine and law, especially since the sixteenth century, will be dealt with in the volume of *The History of Sexuality** that will be devoted to hermaphrodites. An exhaustive documentation, like the one that was made for Pierre Rivière,† will not be found here.

1. First and foremost, a part of Alexina's recollections are missing. Auguste Tardieu seems to have received the complete manuscript from the hands of Dr. Régnier, who had reported the death and performed the autopsy. He kept it, publishing only the part that seemed important to him. He neglected the recollections of Alexina's final years—everything that in his opinion consisted only of laments, recriminations, and incoherencies. In spite of research, it has not been possible to rediscover the manuscript that Tardieu had in his possession. Hence, the present text reproduces what he published in the second part of his work, *La Question de l'identité.***

---

* Michel Foucault, *The History of Sexuality*, volume 1 (New York: Pantheon Books, 1978).

† *I, Pierre Rivière, having slaughtered my mother, my sister, and my brother . . .* , edited by Michel Foucault (New York: Pantheon Books, 1975).

** *Question médico-légale de l'identité dans ses rapports avec les vices de conformation des organes sexuels* (Paris, 1874). The first part of the volume had appeared in the *Annales d'hygiène publique et de médecine légale* in 1872.

2. In the archives of the department of Charente-Maritime there exist a number of documents (several emanating from the office of the superintendent of schools) in which the name of Adélaïde Barbin is mentioned. It seemed to me that it was enough to publish the most significant ones.

3. Medical literature of the end of the nineteenth century and the beginning of the twentieth century refers to Alexina rather often. I have left out what were simply quotations borrowed from the text that was published by Tardieu. I have reproduced only the original reports.

4. As it is known, there was an abundance of "medico-libertine" literature in the final years of the century. Clinical observations sometimes served as inspiration. The story of Alexina can easily be made out in a whole section of the strange novel entitled *L'Hermaphrodite*, which was published in 1899 under the signature of Dubarry.

NAMES, DATES, AND PLACES

Adélaïde Herculine Barbin was born on November 8, 1838, in Saint-Jean-d'Angély. She was usually called Alexina. The first name Camille seems to have been a convention that was invented either by Tardieu, when he published Alexina's recollections, or—more probably—by herself, which allows us to suppose that she was thinking of possible readers.

Certain initials can be more or less easily deciphered.

. . . . .

1838–1853

Childhood in L., that is to say, Saint-Jean-d'Angély.

From 1845 to 1853 she stayed first at the hospital, then at the convent of the Ursulines of Chavagnes.

1853–1856

Stay in B., which is La Rochelle.

1856–1858

Stay at the normal school of Oléron, which was directed by the order of the Filles de la Sagesse. It was located in D., which is Le Château. The directress, whom Alexina calls Sister Marie-des-Anges, was named Sister Marie-Augustine.

T., the goal of the walk that is related on pages 33–39, was Saint-Trojan.

1858–1860

Schoolmistress at L. It has not been possible to identify this canton seat at the extreme limit of the department.

1860

Return to La Rochelle.

The bishop whom Alexina visited was Monseigneur J.-F. Landriot. Consecrated Bishop of La Rochelle on July 20, 1856, he later became the Archbishop of Reims.

The prefect was J.-B. Boffinton, who was installed on December 24, 1856.

The doctor of La Rochelle who made the first report was Dr. Chesnet. His report, which was published in 1860 in the *Annales d'hygiène publique*, is reproduced here on pages 124–28.

The presiding judge of the court of Saint-Jean-d'Angély, who decreed (July 22, 1860) the change of civil status, was named de Bonnegens.

REPORTS

In his Question médico-légale de l'identité dans ses rapports avec les vices de conformation des organes sexuels, *Auguste Tardieu presents Alexina B.'s recollections as follows:*

. . . . .

The extraordinary case that remains for me to report indeed furnishes the most cruel and painful example of the fatal consequences that can proceed from an error committed at the time of birth in the establishment of civil status. We are about to see the victim of such an error, who, after spending twenty years in the clothing of a sex that was not his own, at the mercy of a passion that was unconscious of itself until the explosion of his senses finally alerted him about the nature of it, had his true sex recognized and at the same time became really aware of his physical disability, whereupon, disgusted with his life, he put an end to it by committing suicide.

This poor wretch, who was brought up in a convent and in boarding schools for girls until the age of twenty-two, who passed his examinations and was provided with the diploma of a schoolmistress, saw his civil status reversed by a judgment of the court of La Rochelle* after the most dramatic and moving circumstances, and could not support the miserable existence that his new and incomplete sex imposed upon him. To be sure, the appearances that are typical of the feminine sex were carried very far in his case, but both science and the law were nevertheless obliged to recognize the error and to recognize the true sex of this young man.

The struggles and disturbances to which this unfortunate person was prey have been described by him in pages that are not surpassed in interest by any romantic novel. It is difficult to read a more harrowing story, told with a truer accent, and even though his narrative may not contain a gripping truth, we have, in the authentic and official documents that I shall annex to it, the proof that it is perfectly exact.

I do not hesitate to publish it almost in full, as I wish to keep the lesson that it contains from being lost. This is doubly precious, on the one hand from the standpoint of the influence that the malformation of the sexual organs exercises upon the emotional faculties and upon psychological health, and on the other hand from the standpoint of the serious individual and social consequences that may be entailed by an erroneous declaration of the sex of a newborn child.

* This is an error. The decision to reverse the record of civil status was in fact reached by the civil court of Saint-Jean-d'Angély. Cf. below, p. 151, (M. F.)

The question of identity; the malformation of the external
genital organs; hypospadias; an error about sex

"I, the undersigned, a doctor of medicine, living in La
Rochelle in the department of Charente-Inférieure, am
making known the following facts for the information of
those who are authorized to know them:

"A baby, born to the married couple B. in Saint-Jean-
d'Angély on November 8, 1838, was entered in the civil
status records as a girl; and although she was registered
under the name of Adélaïde-Herculine, her parents made a
habit of calling her Alexina, a name that she has continued
to bear until the present time. Alexina was sent to schools
for girls and later to the normal school of the department of
Charente-Inférieure, where she obtained a teaching certificate
two years ago; she practices her profession in a boarding
school.

"As she had complained of sharp pains she felt in her left
groin, it was decided that she should undergo examination
by a doctor, who could not refrain from expressing his surprise when he saw her genital organs. He confided his observations to the mistress of the boarding school, who tried
to calm Alexina by telling her that what she felt had to do
with her constitution, and that there was nothing to worry
about.

"Alexina, however, preoccupied by a kind of mystery that
centered around herself, as she surmised, and by certain
remarks that the doctor had let slip out in the course of his
examination, began to observe herself more attentively than

she had done before. In daily contact with girls from fifteen to sixteen years old, she experienced emotions that she had difficulty in denying herself. At night, her dreams were sometimes accompanied by indefinable sensations; she felt wet, and in the morning she found grayish and starchy stains on her linen. Surprised as much as she was alarmed, Alexina confided her so completely new sensations to a clergyman who, no less astonished no doubt, urged her to take advantage of a journey that she was to make to B., where her mother lives, in order to consult the Monseigneur. She did, in fact, present herself at the bishopric, and after this visit I was charged with examining Alexina carefully and with giving my opinion concerning her true sex. The following facts resulted from this examination:

"Alexina, who is in her twenty-second year, has brown hair. Her height is one meter fifty-nine centimeters [five feet two inches]. Her features have nothing that is very distinctive and remain sexually indeterminate, being neither those of a man nor those of a woman. Her voice is ordinarily that of a woman, but sometimes in conversation or when she coughs, heavy, masculine tones mingle with it. Her upper lip is covered by a light down; a few beard hairs are to be observed on her cheeks, especially the left one. Her chest is that of a man; it is flat and without a trace of breasts. Menstruation has never occurred, to the great despair of her mother and of the doctor whom she consulted, who saw all his skill remain powerless to bring about the appearance of this periodic discharge. Her upper limbs have nothing of the rounded shapes that characterize those of a well-formed woman: they are very brown and slightly hairy. Her pelvis, her hips, are those of a man.

"The suprapubic region is padded with very abundant

black hair. If her thighs are drawn apart, one perceives a longitudinal groove that reaches from the suprapubic eminence to the vicinity of the anus. On the upper part is to be found a penial body, four to five centimeters [one and a half to two inches] long from its point of insertion to its free extremity, which has the form of a glans covered with a prepuce, slightly flat underneath and imperforate. This little member, which because of its dimensions is as far removed from the clitoris as it is from the penis in its normal state, can, according to Alexina, swell, harden, and lengthen. Nevertheless, the erection, properly speaking, must be very limited, as this imperfect penis is held back on the under side by a sort of frenum that leaves only the glans free.

"The apparent labia majora that can be observed on either side of the groove are very prominent, especially on the right, and they are covered with hair. In reality, they are only the two halves of a scrotum that remained divided. As a matter of fact, by palpating them one plainly feels in each of them an ovoid body suspended from a spermatic cord. It appears to us that these bodies, which are a bit less developed than they are in an adult man, can be nothing other than testicles. The one on the right has completely descended. The one on the left has remained higher; but it is mobile, and it descends more or less when it is pressed. These two globular bodies are very sensitive to pressure when it is somewhat firmly applied. To all appearances, it was the belated passage of the testicle through the abdominal ring that caused the sharp pains Alexina complained about and that necessitated the examination of a doctor, who, when he learned that Alexina did not menstruate, cried out; 'I can very well believe it, and she never will!'

"A centimeter [four-tenths of an inch] below the penis

lies the opening of a urethra that is completely feminine; I introduced a probe into it and allowed a small quantity of urine to flow out. After withdrawing the probe, I urged Alexina to urinate in my presence, which she did, making a vigorous jet that left the canal in a horizontal direction. It is very probable that the sperm must also be cast quite far.

"Below the urethra and about two centimeters [eight-tenths of an inch] above the anus lies the orifice of a very narrow canal, into which I could perhaps have inserted the tip of my little finger if Alexina had not withdrawn and had she not appeared to be in pain. I introduced into it the probe I use for women and discovered that this canal was nearly five centimeters [two inches] long and ended in a cul-de-sac. Introducing my index finger into the anus, I felt the tip of the probe through the walls, which may be called recto-vaginal.

"This canal is therefore a kind of adumbration of a vagina, at the bottom of which there is to be found no vestige of a cervix uteri. Though I thrust my finger far up into the rectum, I could not make out a womb through the walls of the intestine. The buttocks and the thighs, on their bottom part, are covered with abundant black hair, like those of a very hairy man. What shall we conclude from the above facts? Is Alexina a woman? She has a vulva, labia majora, and a feminine urethra, independent of a sort of imperforate penis, which might be a monstrously developed clitoris. She has a vagina. True, it is very short, very narrow; but after all, what is it if it is not a vagina? These are completely feminine attributes. Yes, but Alexina has never menstruated; the whole outer part of her body is that of a man, and my explorations did not enable me to find a womb. Her tastes, her inclinations, draw her toward women. At night she has voluptuous sensations that are followed by a discharge of sperm; her linen is stained and starched with it. Finally, to sum up the matter, ovoid bodies and spermatic cords are found by touch in a divided scrotum. These are the real proofs of sex. We can now conclude and say: Alexina is a man, hermaphroditic, no doubt, but with an obvious predominance of masculine sexual characteristics. In its essential features, his history is almost the exact reproduction of a case that is related by Marc in the article "Hermaphrodite" in the *Dictionnaire des sciences médicales*, and that is also cited by Orphée in the first volume of his *Médecine légale*. Marguerite-Marie, of whom these authors speak, succeeded in having her sexual identification rectified on the civil status records by appealing to the court of Dreux."

E. GOUJON

**A study of a case of incomplete
hermaphroditism in a man***

PRELIMINARY INFORMATION

In the course of the month of February 1868, a young man who was employed in a railroad administration committed suicide by asphyxiating himself with carbon dioxide in a wretched room located on the sixth floor of a house in the rue de l'Ecole-de-Médecine. Doctor Régnier, a doctor in the civil status registry office, and the police superintendent of the quarter were informed of this event, whereupon they went to the home of this unfortunate person and on a table

* *Journal de l'anatomie et de la physiologie de l'homme,* 1869, pp. 609–39.

found a letter that he had left, in which he said that he killed himself in order to escape the sufferings that constantly obsessed him. Suspecting nothing from the outward appearance of the corpse or the information that they picked up from the concierge of the house, who saw this young man every day, that might explain the sufferings to which he alluded, these gentlemen had the idea of examining the genital organs, supposing that he might have been stricken with syphilis, which, as is known, often plunges its victims into a state of deep apathy and great moral prostration, and very often drives to suicide some people who are already melancholic by nature.

On making this examination, Doctor Régnier immediately saw a very great anomaly in the external genital organs and recognized one of the most typical cases of masculine hermaphroditism. In fact, it is difficult, as will be seen later on, to discover a more extreme mixture of the two sexes, as concerns everything relating to the external genital organs. I was informed about this situation by Doctor Duplomb, who regretted as well as myself that science was going to lose the opportunity to make a study of it, and together we requested Doctor Régnier to use all his influence with the police superintendent so that I might be permitted to perform the autopsy and to remove the different parts on which the anomaly had a bearing. This authorization was granted to me on condition that a doctor having an official position would assist me; Doctor Houel was then notified. He was an associate of the Faculty, whom I must thank along with Doctor Régnier for generously turning over to me the study of this remarkable case.

The observation that I am reporting here is certainly one of the most complete that science possesses of this kind, since the individual who is the object of it could be followed, so to speak, from his birth until his death, and since the examination of his corpse, as well as the autopsy, could be performed with all the care to be desired. This observation is especially complete because of the exceptional fact that the person in question took the trouble to leave us long memoirs, through which he initiates us into all the details of his life and all of his experiences during the different periods of his physical and intellectual development. These memoirs* have all the more value because they come from an individual who was gifted with a certain education (he had a teaching certificate and had come out first in the normal school's competitive examination for obtaining this diploma), and he made efforts to describe the particular circumstances of his life.

This individual's situation is not without parallel. In fact, observations are to be found in Geoffroy Saint-Hilaire that have a great analogy to the one that I am reporting.† The hermaphrodite who concerns us was entered in the civil status records as belonging to the feminine sex; he was brought up with girls, among whom he spent his childhood and his adolescence. Physical modifications that later occurred forced him to request a rectification of his civil status, which decisively recognized his sex, which was masculine, although one was more disposed, through a superficial examination of his external genital organs, to classify him among women. Here, moreover, is a passage from his memoirs in which he

---

* Professor Tardieu, having become the owner of these memoirs, has consented, with his customary kindness, to impart them to me.

† See I. Geoffroy Saint-Hilaire, *Histoire des anomalies de l'organisation* (Paris, 1836), in–8°, t. II, p. 30 and following, and atlas, illustration IV.

rapidly enumerates his different positions: "My arrival in Paris marks the beginning of a new phase of my double and bizarre existence.

"Brought up for twenty years among girls, I was at first and for two years at the most a *lady's maid*. When I was sixteen and a half I entered the normal school of . . . as a student-teacher. When I was nineteen I obtained my teaching certificate. A few months later I was directing a rather well-known boarding school in the arrondissement of . . . I left it when I was twenty-one. That was in the month of April. At the end of the same year I was in Paris, with the railroad of . . . "

The autopsy permitted a rectification of the first judgment, which had determined his sexual identity during the greater part of his life, and a confirmation of the exactness of the diagnosis that in the end had assigned him to his true place in society.

According to the preceding statement, it can be seen that the present case raises several physiological and medicolegal questions. The formation of the external genital organs of this individual permitted him, although he was manifestly a man, to play either the masculine or the feminine role in coitus, without distinction; but he was sterile in both cases. He could play the role of the man in this act by virtue of an imperforate penis that was capable of erection, in which state is attained the size it sometimes has in individuals who are regularly formed.

As we shall see later when it is described, this organ was a large clitoris rather than a penis; in fact, among women we sometimes see the clitoris attain the size of the index finger. As he tells us in his memoirs, it was possible for the erection to be accompanied by an ejaculation and voluptuous sensations. This ejaculation was not made by the penis, which was imperforate, as I said above. A vagina ending in a cul-de-sac, into which one could insert the index finger without resistance, allowed him to play the feminine role also in the act of coitus. To this vagina, which was located where it ordinarily is in a woman, were annexed two vulvovaginal glands that opened at the vulva, one on either side, and each next to a little duct that served for the emission or ejaculation of sperm.

I had made the anatomical description of the subject who concerns us when I learned from Professor Tardieu that this unfortunate person had been the object of a medicolegal report by a distinguished doctor of La Rochelle at the time when the court was to pronounce the judgment that was to modify his civil status by recognizing his true sex. As this report is very exact and very well done, I am presenting it in full, and I shall have little to add to it regarding everything that relates to the external genital organs, except, however, a few modifications that came about during the time between the two examinations. Here is the report.*

At the time when I undertook the examination of the corpse, the report that has just been read had been in existence for eight years, and the individual who is the object of it was in his thirtieth year. This is the state in which he appeared then, this poor wretch, who was found in a miserable little room, one of the many that unfortunately still exist in Paris but which the incessant progress of hygiene will perhaps do away with. A mean bed, a small table, and a chair made up

* Here Goujon cites Chesnet's report, which is reproduced on pages 124 to 128. (M. F.)

all the furniture in this place, which could hardly hold four people. A little earthenware stove, in which only ashes were left, stood in a corner next to a rag containing charcoal. The corpse was lying on its back on the bed, partly dressed; the face was cyanosed, and there was a discharge of black and frothy blood coming out of the mouth. Its size was the same as that noted in Doctor Chesnet's report; the hair was black, rather abundant, and fine; the beard was also black, but it was not very abundant on the sides of the face; it was much thicker on the chin and upper lip. The neck was thin and rather long, and the larynx did not protrude very much. The voice, according to information gathered from people who used to see him, had not been very resonant. The chest had the ordinary dimensions and formation of that of a man his size, and no hair was to be found on it, except in the area around the nipples, which were dark and not very prominent; as for the breasts, they were no bigger than those of the average man of this weight.

The lower and upper limbs were covered with very fine black hair, and their muscular development was more clearly defined than it is in a woman. The knees did not turn toward each other; the feet and hands were small; the pelvis was no more developed than it should be in a man.

STATE OF THE EXTERNAL GENITAL ORGANS

On the pubis, which was prominent, there was an abundance of long, curly black hairs, which also covered the perineum and the parts that simulated the labia majora, and completely surrounded the anus; this arrangement is generally missing in a woman. In the place that it normally occupies was to be seen a regularly inserted penis five centimeters [two inches] long and two and one-half centimeters [one inch] in diameter in the state of flaccidity. This organ ended in an imperforate glans that was flattened on the sides and completely exposed by the prepuce, which formed a crown at its root. This penis, which in size did not exceed the clitoris of some women, was slightly curved underneath, held back as it was in that position by the lower part of the prepuce, which merged and vanished into the folds of skin that formed the labia majora and the labia minora.

A bit below the penis was found a urethra analogous to a woman's in position and form. It was easy to introduce a probe into it and to reach the bladder, which we emptied in that way. Below the urethra could be seen the orifice of the vagina, and at the time we made this examination, a slight discharge of blood was coming out of the vulva; Doctor Régnier, who also noted it, believed that it had been caused by probing the vagina with a finger several times in succession at that time.

This is the only explanation, in fact, that is in keeping with this phenomenon; the subject in question, as it was seen above, had never had periodical discharges of blood through the vulva, and the examination of the internal organs explained very well why such discharges had not occurred. One could easily penetrate the full length of the vagina with an index finger, but one could feel nothing at the tip of the finger that recalled the formation of a cervix uteri; on the contrary, one had the feeling of a cul-de-sac.

This vagina was six and one-half centimeters [two and one-half inches] long; upon the sides of it and along its whole length one could make out by touch two hard little cords located beneath the mucous membrane; as we shall see later, these were the ejaculatory ducts, which opened at the vulvar orifice, one on either side. The mucous membrane of the vagina was smooth and very congested. Examination showed that it was covered entirely by a pavement epithelium, which is the kind that lines the normal vagina. It was noted that little follicles existed in the thickness of this mucous membrane. Some circular folds in the membrane were found near the vulvar orifice, but their arrangement did not remind one of a hymen. In the space between the folds of the prepuce, which held the glans in a downward position, and the vulvar orifice, one discovered many small orifices of excretory canals of glands located beneath. By lightly pressing the skin of this region, one could squeeze out of these little holes a gelatinous, colorless matter that was nothing other than solid mucus.

The anus, which was located three and one-half centimeters [an inch and one-half] from the vulva, was in no way abnormal. On either side of the erectile organ (penis or clitoris), forming a groove in which this organ stood, was a voluminous fold of skin. These folds were the two lobes of a scrotum that remained divided. The right lobe, which was much larger than the left one, obviously contained a testicle of normal size, whose spermatic cord could easily be perceived through the skin, right up to the abdominal ring. The left testicle had not completely descended; a large part of it was still caught in the ring.

EXAMINATION OF THE INTERNAL ORGANS

Upon opening the body, one saw that only the epididymis of the left testicle had passed through the ring; it was smaller than the right one; the vasa deferentia drew near each other behind and slightly below the bladder, and had normal connections with the seminal vesicles. Two ejaculatory canals, one on each side of the vagina, protruded from beneath the mucous membrane of the vagina and traveled from the vesicles to the vulvar orifice. The seminal vesicles, the right one being a little larger than the left, were distended by sperm that had a normal consistency and color. A microscopic examination of this liquid, whether it was taken from the vesicles or the testicles, did not show any spermatozoa. However, in the testicle that had passed through the ring and the corresponding vesicle, one saw voluminous rounded bodies that recalled the mother cells of spermatozoa. It was easy to unroll the testicular tubes of both testicles, and the microscope showed nothing abnormal as regarded the one on the right side; but the tubes of the one on the left, which was partly in the abdomen, were fatty and the parenchyma of the testicle had a yellowish tint that the other did not have.

A small cannula having been placed in each of the seminal vesicles, I injected milk into them in order to make sure of the direction of the ejaculatory ducts; this milk jetted out of the orifice of the vulva, on either side, as I said above. The bladder, which was regularly located, was voluminous; distended by an injection of water, it rose up above the pubis. There was nothing that by its form reminded one of a uterus and ovaries. Well above the cul-de-sac that formed the vagina, one found a thick, fibrous surface to which the seminal vesicles clung, and which rose very high up behind the bladder and held the vagina fixed on either side, recalling up to a certain point the form of broad ligaments; but the most careful dissection did not permit one to establish any identification with a uterus or ovaries. It was impossible, moreover, to discover any orifice at the bottom of the vagina; it ended completely in a cul-de-sac.

The peritoneum had normal connections with the bladder and passed way above the vaginal cul-de-sac, which it was far from touching.

At the dissection, one readily noted the presence of two vulvovaginal glands of normal volume and position, and their little excretory ducts, which opened slightly below the canals that ejaculated sperm; when these glands were squeezed, a rather large quantity of viscous liquid was emitted.

On the urethra and in the vicinity of the vesical neck there was also found a little gland that was doubtlessly an undeveloped prostate.

DISCUSSION OF THE PRECEDING FACTS

Although it seems extraordinary that a mistake about the sex of an individual could be protracted for such a long time, science nevertheless has records of a rather large number of such mistakes, some of which have the greatest analogy with the one that concerns us. It is accurate to say that most of these cases had not been the object of a careful examination on the part of doctors, and that it was most often a fortuitous circumstance that provided the physiological demonstration of the true sex. One recalls the case "cited in connection with a report by Geoffroy Saint-Hilaire, of a hermaphrodite monk who had been regarded as a man but who, despite his vows of chastity, revealed by having a baby that his sex was not the same as that of his companions of the cloister." (L. Le Fort, *Vices de conformation des organes génitaux*.)

Schweikhard also reports the story of an individual who was registered as a girl and was regarded as such until the time when he asked for permission to marry a girl who had been made pregnant by him. In this individual the glans was imperforate and the urethra opened beneath it; as it came out, the urine followed the horizontal direction of the penis. The author does not say in this case whether he had ascertained the place from which the sperm was emitted.

Louis Casper, in a work analyzed by Martini, relates that "upon the complaint of a pregnant woman, who accused a midwife of having violated her, the midwife was examined. It was ascertained that her clitoris, although it was more developed than usual, did not have the dimensions adequate for engaging in intercourse; that the vagina was so narrow that only the tip of the little finger could be inserted into it, and that there was a little tumor on one side of it, which suggested the existence of a testicle."

It would be easy to multiply examples of this kind, and it would even be profitable to science if all the documents that it possesses on this question were brought together in a collective work, which would become a precious guide for doctors who are called on to give their opinion and pronounce a judgment concerning people who have been stricken with this kind of anomaly. It would be readily apparent from this work, according to the observations we possess, that if it is sometimes difficult and even impossible to identify the true sex of an individual at the time of birth, it is not the same at a more advanced age, and especially at the approach of puberty. In fact, at this time, inclinations and habits of their true sex are revealed in people who have been victims of an error, and observing these traits would help considerably in marking out their place in society, if the state of the genital organs and their different functions were not sufficient for attaining this end.

This collection of observations would also show clearly—if it was still necessary to demonstrate it—the fact that hermaphroditism does not exist in man and the higher animals.

Surgery is often all-powerful in remedying certain malformations that are designated under the name of hermaphroditism, and several very remarkably successful cases are reported in the thesis of Léon Le Fort: among others, the case taken from the practice of Doctor Huguier, concerning Louise D., for whom this surgeon made an artificial vagina with complete success. One recalls the observation that was made of Marie-Madeleine Lefort, about whom Béclard was charged with making a report in 1815 and who died in 1864 in the Hôtel-Dieu hospital. In spite of Béclard's very exact report, which concluded that she was a woman, for forty years most of the doctors and surgeons of the hospitals in which she was a patient who were able to observe her in the different medical departments where she appeared nevertheless regarded her as belonging to the masculine sex. The autopsy, which was made by Doctor Dacorogna, an intern in the department where Marie-Madeleine Lefort died, demonstrated that Béclard was right. She possessed all the attributes proper to the sex which he had designated to her, differing from other women merely because of a clitoris that was bigger than it should have been and an imperforate vagina that was sealed by a thin membrane. In fact, a simple incision of this membrane would have been enough to restore her permanently to her sex. Béclard, moreover, had proposed that operation when he made his examination.

For a long time many different reasons were put to use in order to explain this kind of anomaly. Comparative anatomy especially has often been invoked; but since the excellent works by Doctor Coste and other modren embryologists, it is above all the anatomy of development, or embryogeny, that we ask for the knowledge necessary to resolve such questions. In fact, it is the study of embryogeny that shows us that the various times of arrest undergone by embryos are the origin of the different deformations or monstrosities that are only too frequently offered to our observation and that in great part constitute pathological anatomy and the entire science of monstrosities, or teratology. I am therefore going to make use of embryogeny in order to explain the state of the external genital organs of the subject of the observation I am reporting. According to Doctor Coste, the external genital organs do not begin to appear until between the fortieth and the forty-fifth day, whereas the corresponding internal organs begin to develop several days earlier. At that fetal period we can observe two small rounded bodies at the top of the little fissure or furrow that lies at the base of the caudal bud. A short while later, this fissure, becoming more and more hollow, will open into the bladder, the vagina, and the rectum. The small rounded bodies later give rise to the corpus cavernosum of the penis in the male and to the clitoris and the labia minora in the female.

These two little eminences join together at their upper edges and form between their lower edges, which remain free, a little groove. This persists in the female but in the male is transformed into a complete canal, which constitutes the urethra. The absence of junction between the free edges of this fissure or groove, in the male, establishes the malformation we designate with the name hypospadias, as in the case of the subject whom we are studying.

Beneath the little eminences I have just spoken about, two others soon develop that are to form the scrotum in the male and the labia majora in the female. Hence, it is the division of the two lobes of the scrotum that constitutes what I have designated as our subject's labia majora.

The analogy that can be established between the different glands that are found in the vagina of the female and those of the urethra of the male perfectly allows us to declare that the vulvovaginal glands of our subject were nothing other than Cowper's or the bulbo-urethral glands; those that existed in the vagina and that ended in a cul-de-sac were the glands of the urethra of the male; this vaginal cul-de-sac was itself nothing other than the canal of the urethra that should have existed under normal conditions.

Professor Courty, who has been much concerned with the organic analogies that exist in the different anatomical systems, justifies in the following very clear and convincing manner the analogies he establishes between the membranous portion of the urethra in the male and the vagina in the female: "The vagina is developed in the blastema that lies between the rectum and the bladder, immediately below the middle perineal aponeurosis—through the formation, in the vesicorectal wall, of a canal that goes to meet the vulvar fissure on one side and the cervix uteri on the other. At exactly the same point and in the same manner the membranous portion of the urethra of the male is formed in front of the urethral crest (the two spermadic ducts back to back), and behind the penile fissure or groove, which before long is converted into a canal by a welding below that is extended inclusively to the bulb.

"From this analogy, which furthermore is confirmed by all sorts of proofs that I do not intend to reproduce here, there follows a consequence that cannot fail to seem paradoxical; namely, first of all, that in the male there is no urethral canal, strictly speaking, while there really is one in the female. In the male, the canal through which the urine flows from the bladder outside is nothing other than the analogue of the vaginovulvar canal of the female, which has been developed in another way and accommodated to other uses. In the male, the urinary passages, strictly speaking, end at the vesical neck. Through its origin and adaptation, the canal that follows it up belongs to the genital system. As a matter of fact, it is above all the propulsor of the semen. It only *lends itself* to the excretion of urine, which runs through it from one end to the other, passing successively into the prostatic (cervix uteri), membranous (vagina), and bulbo-cavernous (vestibule) portions: new proof of the differences of structure or purpose that nature is able to impart to organs that are fundamentally identical."*

The location of the ejaculatory canals in the subject of the observation I am reporting agrees with Professor Courty's theory. We see, in fact, that if this urethra that was transformed into a vagina had developed normally, the external orifices of those little canals would have corresponded to the location of the verumontanum.

Among the medicolegal questions that may be raised by

---

* A. Courty, *Maladie de l'utérus et de ses annexes* (Paris, 1867), in–8°, p. 37.

the kind of observation that was made of Alexina is one that concerns fitness for marriage and reproduction, about which an expert might be called on to give his opinion. One might surely be perplexed by having to make a judgment on such a matter; but I do not believe that one would be sufficiently authorized, after a serious examination of the genital organs, to decide negatively in either the one case or the other.

Procreation is the natural goal of marriage, and Alexina possessed the organs that are characteristic of his sex and whose functions he exercised. The arrangement of the ejaculatory canals was opposed to the semen's being carried directly to the bottom of the vagina; but it is very well known today that fecundation can be brought about even when the seminal fluid impregnates only the entrance of the vagina. Science possesses numerous observations of subjects stricken with hypospadias, whose external urethral orifice was more or less close to the scrotum but who nevertheless fathered several children; and in such cases, the authenticity of paternity was demonstrated by the hereditary transmission to their children of malformations with which they themselves were stricken. The seminal fluid that was taken from the vesicle corresponding to the descended testicle of the subject of our observation did not contain spermatozoa. With all the more reason, the sperm taken from the vesicle of the testicle that had remained caught in the abdominal ring had to be devoid of them likewise,* and that seems to be the rule for testicles that do not carry out their complete

---

* Follin has also reported the observation of individuals who had only one testicle in the scrotum and in whom no spermatozoa were to be found on either one side or the other. (See also the researches of Godard, *Sur la monorchidie et la cryptorchidie*, 1 vol. in-8°, 1860, and *Comptes rendus et mémoires de la Société de biologie*, 1859, with plates.)

migration; but this state of affairs might well have been only temporary for Alexina's testicle that had completely descended, and at another time one might well have noted the presence of spermatozoa in his seminal fluid. It is very well known that in men who have every appearance of health, spermatozoa are sometimes absent for a given time because of one influence or another, and that they may reappear afterward. That might well have been the case for the subject whom we have studied. Contrary to Follin's cases, the numerous and interesting observations of monorchidism reported by E. Godard constantly demonstrate the presence of spermatozoa in the seminal fluid of individuals who had only one testicle in the scrotum.

THE PRESS

L'ECHO ROCHELAIS, *18 July 1860*

As they are talking about nothing else in our town but a strange, an extraordinary metamorphosis in medical physiology, we are going to say a few words about it, according to information taken from a good source.

A twenty-one-year-old girl, a schoolmistress who is as remarkable for the lofty feelings of her heart as she is for her solid education, had lived piously and modestly until today in ignorance of herself, that is to say, with the belief that she *was* what she appeared to be in everybody's opinion, even though for people of experience there were organic peculiarities that should have given rise to astonishment, then doubt, and, through doubt, to understanding; but the girl's Christian upbringing was an innocent blindfold that veiled the truth from her.

At last, very recently, a chance circumstance cast a certain doubt in her mind; an appeal was made to science and an error of sex was recognized. . . . The girl was, quite simply, a young man.

INDÉPENDANT DE LA CHARENTE-INFÉRIEURE, 21 *July 1860*

For some days they have been talking in La Rochelle about nothing else but a singular metamorphosis that has just been undergone by a twenty-one-year-old schoolmistress. This girl, who has a reputation for her talents no less than for her modesty, last week suddenly appeared dressed as a man in the church of Saint-Jean, between her mother and one of the town's most respectable ladies. Some people who had come to attend the mass, surprised by such a travesty in such a place and in such company, and being even less able to explain it on the part of persons who are known for their piety, could not restrain themselves from leaving the church in order to spread the news. Soon the whole quarter was in a flurry; groups were formed; all of them, looking in vain for the key to the enigma, gave themselves up to the most bizarre conjectures; the most preposterous stories circulated throughout the town, but the flower of the gossip blossomed above all right in the middle of the Saint-Jean quarter, where, as it is known, the soil could not be more favorable for it. As it was impossible for us to find our bearings in the midst of such diverse rumors that reached our ears, we abstained from providing our readers with the facts before we fully knew them. This is what results from information drawn from a good source:

It is a matter here of one of those deceptive sexual appearances, which only certain anatomical peculiarities can explain. Medical books contain more than one example of them. The error is even more prolonged because a pious and modest upbringing keeps you in the most honorable ignorance. One day some chance circumstance gives rise in your mind to doubt; an appeal is made to medical science; the error is recognized; and a court delivers a judgment that rectifies your birth record on the civil status registers.

This is the whole story—we shall no longer say, of our young schoolmistress, but of our young fellow citizen. It is a very simple story that can only win him the esteem and interest of all who know him.

DOCUMENTS

Department of Charente-Inférieure
City of La Rochelle

We, Mayor of the city of La Rochelle, Chevalier of the Legion of Honor, upon the attestation that has been given to us by Monsieurs Loyzet, Bouffard, and Basset, who are all three of them members of the Municipal Council,

Certify that Mademoiselle Barbin Adélaïde Herculine, who was born in Saint Jean d'Angély, in the department of Charente-Inférieure, on 7 November 1838, has a good character and is worthy, because of her moral conduct, to devote herself to teaching.

In conformity to Article 4 of the law of 28 June 1833 on primary education, we have granted her the present certificate for her rightful use.

> La Rochelle, 9 June 1856
> The Mayor

. . . . .

The undersigned, the curé of Saint Jean de la Rochelle, certifies that Mademoiselle Alexina Barbin, my parishioner, has always conducted herself in the most edifying way in all respects.

> Guilbaud, priest
> La Rochelle, 7 July 1856

. . . . .

Dear Superintendent,

You had made us hope that we would have the honor of seeing you in the course of last month. I had proposed to present to you Mademoiselle Alexina Barbin, in order to have her admitted to the number of the scholarship students, for her diligence, her intelligence, and her good will make me hope and, so to speak, give me the assurance that in a year she will be able to obtain the teaching certificate. Will you please, dear Superintendent, take an interest in the sorry position of her mother and ask the Prefect to give this young person the place left vacant by Mademoiselle Rivaud, who is in our house in the capacity of an assistant teacher?

Our students are working in earnest, especially on everyday spelling. I am employing all the methods that you had the kindness to point out to me, and I am having them learn the words of the dictionary by heart. Be good enough, dear Superintendent, to come soon and give us your excellent advice. We shall take real pleasure in following it exactly so as to procure a better result for our dear students.

Accept the profound respect of one who has the honor of being, dear Superintendent, your very humble

> Sister Marie-Augustine
> Fille de la Sagesse
> 20 November 1856

. . . . .

Dear Reverend Mother,

From day to day I promise myself the pleasure of going to have a talk with you, but every day I am obliged to postpone this visit because of my work, which absorbs all my time.

I am happy to learn that your students are profiting from your excellent lessons, and I do not doubt that at the next examinations they will make up for the failure that caused us so much distress.

I know about Mademoiselle Barbin's position, which is worthy of interest, and I am very pleased to hear that she has made progress; I do not doubt that the Prefect will consent to grant her a scholarship as soon as possible.

Accept, etc.

. . . . .

Dear Superintendent,

I have learned from my good teacher about your benevolent intention to concern yourself with having me admitted as soon as possible to the number of the scholarship students. Therefore, dear Superintendent, I am asking you to have my nomination accepted by the Prefect for the first of January, and to count upon my being very thankful. My teacher has not corrected my letter, so that you may form your own opinion of my knowledge.

Accept, dear Superintendent, the assurance of my profound respect and my profound gratitude.

> Your very humble servant,
> Alexina Barbin
> Le Château, 18 December 1856

. . . . .

Dear Superintendent,

Mademoiselle Couillaud has written to us that she was returning to Saintes as an assistant teacher in the same boarding school where she was before the examinations. Since the vacation period we have had only eleven scholarship students, whose names are as follows: Mademoiselles Clarisse Bonnin, Offélia Masseau, Céline Peslier, Rosa Bouchaud, Elisa Pellerin, Elisa Jaquaud, Françoise Menant, Clémentine Murat, Adèle Besson, Marie-Thérèse Turaud, and Amélie Lemarié. I hope, dear Superintendent, that you will choose to complete the number by admitting Mademoiselle Barbin, whose capacity you have been able to judge. . . .

We regret, dear Superintendent, that your numerous

occupations are depriving us for so long of the honor of seeing you.

I have the honor of being, with the most profound respect, dear Superintendent, your very humble servant,

Sister Marie-Augustine
Fille de la Sagesse

. . . . .

No. 145 *The Birth of Adélaïde Herculine Barbin*

In the year one thousand eight hundred and thirty eight, on the eighth of November, at three o'clock in the afternoon, before us, Jean Baptiste Joseph Marie Chopy, the mayor and civil status registrar of the commune of Saint Jean d'Angély, in the canton of Saint Jean d'Angély, in the department of Charente-Inférieure, appeared Jean Barbin, twenty-two years of age, residing in Saint Jean d'Angély, a sabot maker by profession, who presented to us a child of the feminine sex, born last night at midnight in the home of the father and mother, rue de Jélu, from the legitimate marriage of himself, the informant, and of Adélaïde Destouches, twenty-two years of age, without profession, residing in this town; to whom he gave the first names Adélaïde Herculine. The said declarations and presentation were made in the presence of Jacques Destouches, the maternal grandfather of the child, fifty years of age, residing in Saint Jean d'Angély, a sabot maker by profession, and of Jean Baptiste Lebrun, twenty-five years of age, residing in Saint Jean d'Angély, a joiner by profession; and the informants and witnesses signed the present certificate with us after it was read to them, except the first, who said he did not know how to sign his name.

(The following note is inscribed in the margin:)

By the judgment of the civil court of Saint-Jean d'Angély dated 21 June 1860, it has been ordained that the record opposite should be rectified in this sense:

1) that the child registered here will be designated as being of the masculine sex;

2) and that the first name Abel shall be substituted for Adélaïde Herculine.

Saint-Jean d'Angély, 22 June 1860

· · · · ·

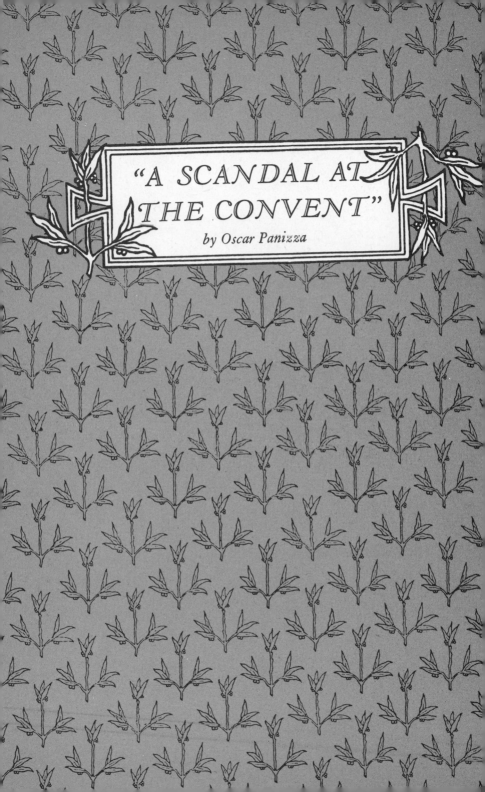

"A SCANDAL AT THE CONVENT"

by Oscar Panizza

. . . male and female created he them. . . .
and God said unto them, Be fruitful, and multiply. . . .

Genesis 1 : 27–28

．　．　．　．　．

In 1830 the secularized convent of Douay in Normandy re-
verted to its original purpose when the government permitted the establishment, in its spacious, ornate rooms, of a
boarding school for young ladies, under the supervision of
an Abbé, together with the necessary number of teachers in
the persons of the Dominican nuns who had been its inmates. Their young charges were drawn from the best
families in the country. The idea was to make certain con-
cessions to the still-aggrieved French nobility and to let
them enjoy in the country certain prerogatives from which
they were debarred in the capital cities, notably Paris, which
they avoided at this time: prestige, the freedom to make a
splendid appearance, and especially a certain influence upon
local institutions and the populace. That such an influence
was consonant with the strengthening of the Catholic disposition lay in the nature of the case. It was quite in the
spirit of the noble ladies who sponsored this convent school
that the young girls were expected to take certain vows upon
admission. This was, first of all, the aristocratic thing to do.
It would also give them a foretaste of the true life of the
cloister, in case some of them should prefer—given the
lowered expectations of suitable marriages—to take the veil

for good. And so vows were taken. Of the well-known three, the vow of poverty was naturally not to be exacted from the noble children, whose parents would come on Sunday visits from their estates, driving two or four horses, and leaving extra allowances for fruit and sweets. The vow of obedience, however, was strictly required, as was the vow of chastity— the girls were all between the ages of fourteen and eighteen. To this last vow we will refer again later. It is not entirely irrelevant to our story.

But first, a brief list of characters in this drama, which the reader may be expected to regard, in the end, as a tragicomedy: To begin, there was the Abbé (de Rochechouard), usually referred to simply as Monsieur l'Abbé, or even just Monsieur, as he was the only man in the convent school, other than the gardener and the sacristan. He was a fine, highly cultivated cleric of ancient lineage, in his fifties, somewhat indolent, perhaps, his position being after all rather a sinecure, not a job. Monsieur was charged with the spiritual offices of the school chapel, aided by an assistant, and with overseeing the little parish church in the village of Beauregard, which was connected with the building complex of the establishment. Monsieur's position, then, was chiefly honorific. He had a good private income and was free to indulge his love for books, though he was not actually driven by any thirst for knowledge. He was a gormandizer who would open this little volume today, another tomorrow, fishing up a few ideas to play with for the rest of the day. He was interested in theology exclusively; the classics were of course not absent from his shelves, nor the few erotic treatises that went with them. Monsieur l'Abbé was no sensualist; his body was too well padded, and his face too good-natured. Nor was he productive. He wrote no commentary on a thesis of Thomas Aquinas and issued no proposals for timely modifications of the spiritual exercises practiced in monastic schools; his was a calm, serene nature, content with whatever the day might bring. He was a cleric right out of the novels of Cherbuliez, a peaceful stroller in the Lord's vineyard who does not criticize the quality of the grapes, neither does he do anything to improve them, pleased to let grow what will. He had a low forehead; short, thick, abundant hair; small, peaceable eyes; full, contented cheeks; a mouth most finely drawn; a stocky figure. He was brief, simple, and sparing of speech, matter-of-fact in tone, by nature disinclined to preach. All in all, he was a creature quietly at work in and for himself; his habit was always immaculate.

Then there was the Mother Superior, usually called only Madame, the female head of the institute, a de Vremy by birth, of an old Norman family. She was an indescribably proud lady well into her forties, sagacious and dignified in the extreme. Even the haughty countesses, mothers of her charges who came on a visit or on business, made obeisance to her, as she expressly demanded; for even apart from her ancient lineage, she was, after all, almost an abbess. Upon the chamois-yellow habit of her order she always wore a golden cross presented to her by the Pope. While officially she ranked below the Abbé, in fact she ranked high above him; she conducted all the complicated business of the institute, thus relieving her spiritual superior, who was most indolent, of a great burden. Accordingly, her relations with the Abbé were excellent, indeed, intimate. She would spend hours in his room conversing privately with him in confidential whispers. Yet there was no hint of sensuality, or even of a sensual inclination, in their tête-à-têtes. In this respect, they were both negatively predisposed. Monsieur was passive, meditative by nature; Madame had a keen mind, and at her age, her emotions having cooled, she was entirely ruled by her intelligence. She did have a passion for literature of the worldly sort, and in addition to using the Abbé's library, in which she alone was free to browse at will, she received a large package of books from Paris every month. When the servants tidied her apartment in the evening, they found it full of a fine, bluish smoke. Oddly enough, Madame, who never taught any classes and attended only morning prayers and other such services in church, was known to detain many of the youngest pupils for hours in her rooms. For the rest, the Mother Superior was seldom seen, seldom spoke, never interfered personally in affairs, received oral reports on everything from the eight sisters of the order, and issued her own commands by way of subordinates, who saw to their execution throughout all the rooms and departments of the cloister's extensive buildings and grounds. Even in the village the least sign from her was an order, and her invisible spirit dominated the world around Douay and far beyond Beauregard.

With the next person on our list we approach the actual conflict which is the subject of our story. Mademoiselle Henriette de Bujac was the niece of Madame de Vremy, the Mother Superior. She was a pretty, lively girl of about seventeen, called Henriette for the most part, with a head of short dark curls, fiery black eyes, a slender figure, and a lively imagination. Actually she was a little past the proper age for submitting to the convent's regimen, but had been admitted because of a domestic problem—an aunt subject to severe fits made Henriette's presence at home inadvisable— and because Madame de Vremy was a close relative. She was called "The White Devil" because she had so many costly white and cream-colored dresses from home, being one of the richest among the girls, and because she was so adroit in her movements and her speech, and was such a versatile mimic. She was, of course, Madame's "naughty darling" and the "insufferable minx" of the Abbé's room. But this exhausts the list of Henriette's allies in the chronic struggle of petty jealousies and shifting allegiances in the feminine world of the cloister. For she was certainly hated by all eight teaching nuns, who could teach her nothing about feminine wiles, and from whom she had no wish to learn the customary studies and disciplines. This hatred vented itself most effectively through the fourth person of our drama, the Head Sister, usually called the Head. A shrewd and sensible lady, she was also of noble birth, the principal teacher of the institute, and first lady of the convent after the Mother Superior, whose presumptive successor she was. Henriette was also hated, however, by most of her fellow pupils because of her white dresses, her advantage in being older than most of the others, and the endless liberties and whims in which she indulged herself.

Before we come to Henriette's relationship to Mademoiselle Alexina Besnard, the true heroine of our story, let us present a quick portrait of Mademoiselle Alexina. That young lady, nearly the same age as Henriette and one of the more remarkable students of the institute, was the most diligent and accomplished girl in the school, its chief ornament, and for many families the model of all that could be accomplished at Douay. Alexina, the child of a very poor family, was from the first a high-spirited and precocious girl, a prizewinner in school, and exceptionally gifted in mathematics and languages. She picked up everything with playful ease, and passed it along with the same light touch to the younger girls she instructed. In this respect she was considered a phenomenon. Such an excess of intellectual prowess was bound to come to the attention of her village priest. One fine morning, with a warm letter of recommendation from him, Alexina's parents came knocking at the portals of Douay, accompanied by their fourteen-year-old daughter. There it took only a brief examination to reveal what they had on their hands. Alexina Besnard was admitted free of charge, and after only one year everyone had agreed to groom this rare talent as a teacher for the convent.

Alexina had only one inadequacy as far as learning was concerned, and that was in feminine needlework of all kinds, which she loathed and refused to touch. But this could hardly be considered an obstacle to her career, as one could find a thousand willing crochet-workers for one mathematician. In appearance, Alexina was certainly odd and different. She was tall and slender, with a rapid, long stride that kept her skirts in ungainly motion. Her face was lean and could have been called homely but for the captivating glance of her keen, quick, piercing, and all-devouring eyes, and the exceptional turn of mind suggested by her aquiline nose, in itself very handsome. The unbecoming convent robes she wore at all times revealed nothing of her physical form, but the chances that she might have cut the figure of an Aphrodite were minimal, especially as she would tolerate no laces, ruffs, or flattering caps to improve her appearance. She could not wait, as she put it, to put on the habit of a nun. Alexina's voice was sharp, a high treble, as if designed to command the younger pupils, but it attracted attention when she was singing in the chorus, because of its tendency to change abruptly to an alto. All in all, she was a veritable rat's nest of odd and exceptional talents and capacities; she also had a crystal-hard multifaceted technique for bending everything around her to her will, honing it to suit herself and her own inclinations.

It was to this poor, strange, brittle, and rather intolerant young woman who, compared with the other children at the institute, had only her brilliant intellectual gifts to weigh in the balance, that Henriette, the rich, spoiled, luxury-loving, well-bred young aristocrat, attached herself from her very first days at the convent. On the day our story begins, after a year of getting to know each other, these two were inseparable companions, with the initiative for this rare, tender relationship decidedly coming from Mademoiselle de Bujac. It is true that Henriette de Bujac was a kind, compassionate young girl who might have been drawn at first to Alexina because of the latter's poverty and her awkward situation at the convent. But Henriette's wealth, her abundant pocket money, her fine clothes were the last things in the world Alexina would or could profit from. So there was not enough here to make so strong a bond between two girls of such a tender age, while Alexina's learning and intellectual powers counted for even less, not being the sort of thing to impress the flighty, lively, fun-loving, and lazy Henriette. Furthermore, her scholastic progress left as much to be desired after the friendship as before it. But how light and diaphanous is the web of sympathy—so mysterious a bond even in ordinary circumstances—when it binds the capricious hearts of young girls. And how easily torn!

And so, with the addition of maidservants, pupils, and white-clad nuns with scapulars, we come to the end of our list of characters. We can let the 20th of June 1831 begin; that day remembered by the cloister walls of Douay, on the evening of which the hundred or hundred and twenty inmates of the institute all, without exception, went to bed with pounding hearts and furrowed brows. Then came one more night; and then, early the following morning, one of nature's most stunning manifestations—but also one of the most atrocious social catastrophes—was brought to a close.

Monsieur l'Abbé sat in his room. He had drunk his breakfast coffee and set the cup aside. Monsieur did not smoke, but he read, and instead of an after-breakfast cigar he was reading Liguori's *Theologiae moralis, libri sex.* Monsieur was most at home in the field of moral theology; authors in that field such as Busenbaum, Ribadeneira, Sanchez, lay close at hand in attractive, pressed-parchment editions. Was Monsieur very moral in life? We have no way of telling, but that has nothing to do with our story. Monsieur enjoyed reading works on morality much as another man might enjoy going hunting, without considering the question of whether he loved killing animals. Monsieur enjoyed turning over moral concepts in his mind. He toyed with the cardinal virtues, experimentally drew specific vices from his treatises, like black vials, and in his imagination carefully injected them into the hearts of people he knew, letting them ferment there, in order to see what might come of it.

Which chapter Monsieur was reading in Liguori, we cannot tell, no matter how hard we try, leaning over his shoulder, to decipher the text, because the print in those seventeenth-century editions, especially the Lyons editions, was so bad, ribbed and crumpled. But he had apparently come to a passage of high interest, because he was blinking his eyes and running his index finger all around his nose, which organ was not too far from the printed page. We have already stated that Monsieur was not a sensual man by nature, so let there be no misunderstanding here: Monsieur was of a lofty disposition, and dwelled impartially on whatever came under his lens for observation. If he happened to be reading *de Verecundia*, it was not shame in the common sense that interested him, but the subtle gradations of *castitas*, chastity; and it was certainly not the feelings of shame experienced by some servant girl that interested him, but the much subtler forms they might take in the angels of heaven.

As we cannot determine in precisely which chapter Monsieur is engrossed, we may as well look around in the Abbé's room for other points of interest. It is a bright, inviting place; the morning sun, its glare softened by heavy green drapes, comes in through the window next to which stands the noble cleric's large, flat work table. On the floor is a handsome tiger skin, with the Abbé's dainty buckled shoes nestling in its folds. At the back, in the direction of the second window, stands a great silk-covered screen, cutting off about a third of the room. When we stand behind the Abbé, we cannot see beyond it; but to the front, lit up by another east window, whose drapes are wholly drawn, we can see four or five bookcases lining the wall, chock-full of volumes whose titles we cannot read at this distance. Judging by their numerous yellowing backs of parchment or pigskin, they must contain quantities of theology. On our left, another little prayer stand; on the same side, two doors, one leading directly to the Mother Superior's apartments one flight up, and another opening on the corridor—the Abbé's front door, in short; another little flower arrangement; a fireplace between the two east windows, with a few statuettes on the mantel; and—to mention the most striking fact last of all— a fascinating, special aroma, such as is always found in the rooms of exceptional people. This was the first thing one noticed on entering Monsieur's room, an aroma compounded of raisins, printer's ink, tiger-skin powder, and the prelate's personal sweat, which clung tenaciously to the room. Wherewith we have introduced our reader to the Abbé's study on the first floor of the convent's main building.

While the Abbé was immersing himself in Liguori's moral problems, the fourteen-, fifteen-, and sixteen-year-old girls on the third floor were pulling on their knickers and getting into their slippers, each making for the wash basin on the stand beside her bed, to splash fresh water over the thin back of her neck, rub her cheeks and forehead a bit, and brush back her hair; for it was seven in the morning, time to get up, and the only reason Monsieur was up so much earlier was that he had to read his morning Mass. The whole dormitory was now a vision of white lights and surfaces, the skintones of bare arms and necks amid the gleaming white of petticoats and camisoles, and sometimes pearly glimmerings between open lips. There were sounds of slippings and slidings, of clothing being pulled off and on, the snapping of garters, the flapping of slippers, the swishing of washcloths. Otherwise all was quiet, because the minds of these young creatures still lay swaddled in their dreams, which kept them from their usual prattling and chattering.

And the Mother Superior? She was probably awake, drinking her morning cocoa, reclining in a bathrobe embroidered with crosses and hearts and nails-of-the-cross, engaged in producing that blue haze in her rooms which the maids always noticed there, and which they took to be incense from Madame's private devotions. Perhaps she was reaching inside the half-opened package from Paris, fetching up a little octavo volume, and beginning to read in it, to read on and on, often until the sun stood high in the heavens. For Madame did not attend the morning prayers that brought all the convent's inmates together before breakfast. She performed no official duties in the mornings. Today she would also have continued to recline in her robe decorated with the symbols of Christ's Passion, and would have finished reading her little octavo volume, had it not been for a sharp whispering at her bedside, bringing her a very strange report indeed.

Meanwhile the seventy or eighty young inmates of the convent, eyes still sticky with sleep, were tramping and slipping and tripping down the stairs and into the great halls on the ground floor where prayer services were held, for their brief morning devotions, to be followed by the longed-for breakfast of much white bread, butter, and coffee.

Even while they were chasing down those stairs, even during prayers, and even more so during breakfast, when the rosebud mouths began to exercise themselves in the gossiping that went on all day long, there was a degree of whispering, hissing, and gesturing most unusual for this ordinarily sleepy morning hour. When, after breakfast, big girls and little girls should have been getting to work at last in their various classrooms, busy with arithmetic, classics, memorizing, theme writing, and calligraphy, it seemed instead that the strangest excitement had seized the whole young bee swarm, that all these hearts and heads were full of an intense ferment; all their eyes were aglitter, their cheeks aglow. And because the Head Sister—far from driving all the young palace revolutionaries off to work with a single wave of her hand, as she could easily have done—smilingly put up with it all, it was no wonder that everything happened as it did.

Monsieur l'Abbé still sat on his tiger rug, reading Liguori,

Theologiae moralis, libri sex. It was long after breakfast, and he, like Madame, had not appeared for morning prayers. But now there was a sudden commotion in the corridor outside his door, a humming and buzzing, a rattling as if an avalanche of little teeth was gathering, a swishing of skirts and aprons, a shuffling of little shoe soles, and stamping, pressing, giggling, and shushing sounds without end. Monsieur recognized these sounds: they were the same sounds he used to hear on a hot midsummer afternoon at two o'clock, when thirty to forty girls would plant themselves at his door and make a racket until he opened it, whereupon the entire company would sink to their knees before him, hands folded, begging for "A heat recess, please, Your Reverence?" But there was no heat yet; nor was it two in the afternoon, but rather nine in the morning; and no one could know whether it was going to be a hot day.

Monsieur was still reading, his right index finger curved around the hook of his nose. He liked to stretch his moral breakfast of Liguori or Aquinas till ten or eleven o'clock. But when the door seemed in danger of being broken down by the tramplings outside, he rose to his feet. He went and opened the door, and the whole horde of young girls in their gray work pinafores, with white puffs of tulle at the shoulders, their unruly hair hidden under dainty little chamois caps, broke into his room. All were shouting at once with indignation, leaning forward, flinging their hands apart only to clap them together again—and the only words Monsieur could make out in this tumult were two names, Henriette and the Schoolmistress, over and over again. "The Schoolmistress" was the name the girls had given Alexina, who had recently been assigned a few classes to teach in the younger ranks. The name had caught on, was now generally accepted, and seemed to serve as a happy augury of her future position in the convent. Now, suddenly, this expression was to take on a shocking new meaning. Monsieur kept hearing only "Henriette" and "the Schoolmistress." At length he called for silence, turned to one of the older girls, and asked what had happened. Now it all came out: This morning when everybody was getting up, Henriette, Madame's niece, had been found in bed with Alexina, her intimate friend, in the older girls' dormitory. They were asleep, their hands and bodies intertwined. Henriette's bed, which stood in another row, was empty. One of the older girls, who had risen early owing to a call of nature, had noticed them, but had gone on her way. When they were still lying there on her return, however, she had awakened some of the other girls, who were equally astonished by what they saw. Others came, awakened by the noise and the giggling, and in the end, half the dormitory's population was standing around the two sleepers, gaping. Then somebody yanked the covers off; and what they saw was horrible. Alexina and Henriette, waking up, separated themselves, screaming.

By now all the girls had made a contribution to this report, their faces aflame. At this point there was a pause. When Monsieur, still holding his little volume of Liguori, one finger of his left hand inserted between the pages to keep his place, his right thumb hooked between two buttons of his clerical gown, merely injected a calm *"Eh bien?"* as if to say, "So—what else?" all the young brats virtually hurled themselves at him with hands uplifted and cried in one voice:

"But it's disgraceful. It's horrible, it's filthy, it's everything foul you can think of!"

The youngsters evidently knew that they could cry out in this fashion without lessening the immense distance separating them from their superior and priest. Monsieur had, as one might say, a broad back on which the little fists could be allowed to drum a tattoo now and then. If he was someone close to *le bon Dieu* for his eighty or a hundred young charges, with their strict religious upbringing, he was also *le bon père*, with all the benevolence implied in that high position; and especially in matters of a specifically feminine nature, the girls were permitted to express themselves in their customary hyperbolic and emotional way. The Abbé noticed that the older girls were also present, standing about looking embarrassed.

The door opened and in came the Head Sister, with a troubled expression on her face, perhaps a shade overemphatic. She fell to her knees close to the Abbé (a permissible dramatic form of expression at the convent), covered her face with her hands and in part with his gown, and sobbed out:

"Oh, Monsieur, how shameful!"

"Come, my dear, what's wrong?" asked the Abbé in a soothing tone. He raised the principal sister, whom he held in highest regard, to her feet. Henriette and Alexina, he was now told, had disappeared. They had not come to morning prayers or to breakfast. This fact, and all sorts of rumors now running through the convent, suggested some unusual, grave infraction on their part.

At this point another contingent of girls came crowding in, with more news they claimed to have heard from the maids. Beyond the half-open door, the maliciously grinning faces of these same women could be seen, listening to make sure their information was properly transmitted: Alexina had been found crouching in her nightshirt up in the attic, and she was refusing to come down unless her clothes were brought up to her. Henriette, too, was found. She had tried to hide in the pantry, but was discovered by the housekeeper, whereupon she had run upstairs, also still in her nightdress, to the Mother Superior's apartment. Madame had then ordered her niece's clothes to be brought to her. It was further noted that Henriette's bed had not been slept in at all last night, but was still undisturbed. Other voices instantly arose to testify that Henriette had often been seen at the ungodliest hours of the morning deliberately rumpling her bedclothes before getting dressed. Clearly the bed had not been slept in at those times, since people did not normally rumple their bed *after* arising from it!

At this moment the second door to Monsieur's room opened and the Mother Superior came in. All the girls fell back, partly out of respect, but also a little as if caught in the act. Only the Head Sister held her ground, facing Madame with a steely eye. From this stare alone and its encounter with Madame's answering look, an initiate could have sized up the entire situation. Had the Abbé been more perceptive, he would have known in that moment that the whole silly schoolgirl crush between Henriette and Alexina, which all the fuss was apparently about, would only provide another testing ground for the two ladies. Henriette, Madame's niece, was to serve as the weak point in Madame's armor, the means of exposing Madame's dubious courses, the weakness of her position, and ultimately the means of driving her off the field.

Madame seemed indignant and expressed surprise at the presence here of all the pupils; was the Day of Judgment at hand? They were all to go at once to their classrooms. At a wave of her hand the whole crowd dispersed. With an assumed air of kindliness she then admonished the Head Sister not to let these aggressive, unruly girls seize the reins of order in the convent. She had heard all about the incident. It was hardly worth mentioning. The culprits would of course have to be taken in hand, but to turn everything in the Convent of Douay topsy-turvy over such a trifle was absurd. She would hold the Head responsible for keeping strict order the rest of the day. With a subdued "Certainly, Reverend Mother," the Head departed, leaving Madame alone with Monsieur.

Thus far the Abbé had come to no decision at all. He preferred to be the silent spectator while registering the facts in his mind. Now, too, he said nothing, but waited for Madame to speak.

"What a ghastly business," she said, showing for the first time how worried she was, not about the thing in itself, but rather the uproar it had caused. That it should have been allowed to take on such dimensions! Why, it was as though the Devil had taken possession of every living soul in the place. Monsieur waved this notion away, making three signs of the cross. Ah well, Madame said, it was really too bad that the thing had been allowed to go so far. Surely, the nuns had been remiss in their duties. The Head Sister would have to be punished, preferably transferred to a sister convent.

"The Head Sister? Ah no!" said Monsieur, quite defensively. He was rather fond of her; she was quite indispensable here as a teacher. Who could replace her, if only in French style? Not to mention her qualities as a supervisor! No! The trouble was that neither he nor Madame ever attended morning prayers or breakfast. Had they done so today, the affair, which had been going on since six or seven, would have been discovered in time. By nine o'clock the whole swarm of bees had already flown. But Madame insisted that the nuns were to blame for the trouble. Children of fifteen, sixteen, would never have worked themselves up to such a pitch unaided.

Monsieur, though, was far more interested in the moral aspects of the case. Did it happen often, then, that girls went to bed together like this? Of course it did, the little creatures were as playful as kittens with each other. Ah, but Henriette was almost seventeen, and the Schoolmistress was going on eighteen, she was in fact already teaching the youngest. Certainly, but the friendship between these two was extraordinarily close. Indeed, the Abbé wondered, and did these friendships between young girls always take so sensual a form? Sometimes, yes. She had not had the slightest hint of the extreme lengths to which these two had gone, but she had heard of such cases. However, there was nothing reprehensible about it; both these girls were after all young, excitable, imaginative. The Abbé made a movement with his hand, as if to indicate that this explanation did not satisfy him, then turned to the bookshelves by the window. In any case, Madame said in leaving, the young flock were back in their cages now. She would hasten to give orders that Alexina and Henriette were to come down to lunch as if nothing had happened. There must be no show of separating the two young sinners. The whole thing might still be smoothed over.

In this she was mistaken. If only the Head had not been so determined to keep the iron hot—it was now glowing with white heat—under any circumstances. If only Monsieur l'Abbé could have suppressed his curiosity about the moral aspects of the matter, and given up lending an ear to every fresh rumor carried to him! He had meanwhile pulled out his Ecclesiastical Dictionary and was reading the entry under "Sappho." When he did not find what he was looking for, he went on to "Lesbos" and, still unfulfilled, he found the article on "Tribadism." This he took with him to his tiger skin and pored over it for a good half-hour.

For a moment, all was quiet. But we cannot give the reader a rest. He must race with us through the whole scandalous affair just as it happened, in the few hours of one afternoon. He must fly with us like a bat out of hell through this Breughel-like witches' sabbath inside a convent. There is no time to dwell on details, not even to pause and catch one's breath.

The convent had a rule that any pupil possessed the right to take a request or complaint directly to the Abbé or the Mother Superior. It was meant to reassure parents and relatives that every precaution was being taken against the abuse of authority by subordinates, but in view of the humane and almost patriarchal discipline, this option was almost never resorted to. The young inmates must have been reminded of this provision by the Head Sister and the other nuns, for when the girls were dismissed from their classes at ten A.M. for the usual fifteen-minute break and the customary thick slice of nourishing black bread, the same swarm that had appeared at the Abbé's door after breakfast gathered there again. Once more a lot of shuffling, stamping, whispering, rattling, scraping, and giggling warned the Abbé, who had been pacing the floor deep in thought with a volume of Sappho's poems in his hands, that more events of a moral nature were in the offing. This case was quite to his taste. He wanted to know just how far a sinful nature could drive innocent young girls to sensual practices in which the Devil certainly was implicated, no matter how lightly, and what sort of problems and sidelights of a theoretical-moral or practical-disciplinary nature might be involved. From this a bold leap took him back to classical antiquity, to the time before the Prince of Darkness had been chained down, when he was free to play his infamous tricks on mankind, such as entrapping pagan women in hopelessly evil courses in the form of "tribadism," a relic of which, a mere thread, still manifested itself in the nineteenth century, even in convents, bearing witness that the power of Evil had not yet been entirely subdued. Et cetera, et cetera. Such were the reflections which so wholly absorbed Monsieur that Madame's diplomatic suggestions not to let the matter go any further had quite gone out of his mind.

And so Monsieur l'Abbé quickly opened the door leading to the hallway, admitted all the girls standing there with their flaming lips and their bread uneaten, and closed the door behind them.

"My children," he said, "I must ask you to speak only one at a time, and not to tell me the same thing twice. Understood?" Whereupon he was inundated by an outpouring of the most hair-raising details which the girls, with the help of the supervising nuns, had dredged up from their memories during the last hour, instead of doing their calligraphy, history, memorizing, arithmetic, and the like: They had been noticing the most peculiar goings-on between the Schoolmistress and Henriette for a long time now. Those two were always thick as thieves, whispering in dark corners, kissing—there was no end to it. Whenever they were seated at some distance apart in class, they were always "making eyes" and signaling to each other. The way they were always chasing after each other, inextricably wrapped up in each other, entangled like two vines, was incredible. Another group said: The Schoolmistress was an odd creature, with something about her like no other girl ever. The Schoolmistress never went bathing with the rest of the girls, but always found some excuse for staying in. She was always bashful about relieving herself in the presence of the other girls, yet she had often been heard to giggle in the water closet when she was there alone with Henriette. Anyway Henriette hadn't slept in her own bed for the last six months, but always slipped in with Alexina, and then got up very early. Alexina did not wear the same kind of underpants as the other girls. She had strange knickers with a slit in the wrong place. Her corset did not fit, she was so bony; and her walk was different, not like a girl's walk at all. In short, the Schoolmistress was a peculiar sort of person, which was why she could do things others couldn't do, and was smarter than all the rest of them put together.

Yet another group, among them the occupant of the bed next to Alexina's, said that Henriette and the Schoolmistress kissed passionately in bed. She had heard them, pretending to be asleep. They embraced and called each other "my darling!" This morning, when the covers had been pulled off them and all the girls were looking on, they had their legs wrapped around each other, with a large part of their bodies quite exposed; and Alexina had coarse limbs and hair all over her legs, like the Devil.

This last remark, accompanied by an "Ugh!" of disgust by the whole chorus, was deprecated by the Abbé on the grounds that it was not established whether the Devil had hairy legs, and, if so, how hairy they were; nor was this a proper subject of conversation for young girls. One of the older girls then deposed as follows: She had seen Mademoiselle Alexina slip a hand under Henriette's skirts, and Henriette had let her do it, though she blushed a dark red. When they noticed the onlooker, though, they both laughed and skipped off together. "How disgusting!" The girls cried in chorus, "oh, how awful!" Finally another of the older girls said she did not think that Alexina was a girl at all; she was much too smart; she knew almost everything; and she wasn't gentle, like other girls, but rough and hard. She felt sure that Alexina was an evil spirit in the semblance of a girl, who would one day vanish all of a sudden, in a cloud of stench and noise.

Monsieur listened calmly to all this and to much more besides. Then he told the girls to go quietly to their next classes, pending investigation of everything they had told him. Meanwhile would they go find the Head Sister and bid her come to him?

"The Head! The Head!" the girls shouted in relief, and stormed out of the room pell-mell.

While these important interrogations and testimonies were going on in Monsieur's study, Madame in her second-story apartment seemed to have recovered her equanimity completely. She did not come down again to see if order had been restored, and her loyal cohorts, who ordinarily could not hasten to her quickly enough—as they had this very morning to impart to her triumphantly the latest news—all seemed to have deserted to the Head Sister's party, like rats from a ship. So the proud, hitherto independent and all-powerful self-styled abbess kept to herself upstairs with her novels and her cigarettes. She had no idea of what was going on below, especially of how excluded she had already become. In the adjoining room sat Henriette and Alexina, somewhat subdued and pensive, to be sure, as a result of all the reprimands and warnings they had certainly received, but otherwise remarkably fresh and relaxed. Henriette, a dazzling little beauty, with that carefree air which is a natural accompaniment of such conquering good looks and of her unassailable position as Madame's niece, had ordered up her prettiest cream-colored frock. There she sat, full of good spirits, ready for anything. Not so Alexina. Not only was her future far less assured in case of a misstep; she also had a certain grasp of the situation. Even though she regarded her relations with Henriette as harmless, innocent, and fully justified, her pious upbringing had sharpened her judgment for what was, after all, improper conduct, particularly for someone like herself who was already on the way to being a teacher. She felt the morally dubious aspects of what had occurred like a vicious stab in her insides. Yet her eyes also betrayed a certain sense of triumph. By sheer will power she had overcome all the obstacles standing in the way of her love for Henriette; her friend was still bound to her with all the fibers of her being.

The time came for the midday meal. This was the only occasion of the day which brought all the cloister's inmates together, except for the maids. The whole procession of young chatterboxes, feverish with excitement and curiosity, poured into the spacious refectory of the old cloister. And now the incredible happened. As Madame entered the dining room with Henriette and Alexina and the two girls made for their customary places at table, their fellow pupils, especially the very young fourteen- and fifteen-year olds, drew back from the two sinners violently, as if in sudden panic, screaming and showing their disgust. They especially turned from Alexina who, as "the Schoolmistress," also supervised a table for the very young. The nuns in full habit did not lift a finger to intervene, and when Madame, with threatening mien, called out, "What is the meaning of this?," attempting to restore the girls to order, there arose such an uproar, to which even the older girls succumbed, that all further resistance was dropped, and the two girls were left to their fate. With a single glance at Madame's face, the perceptive Alexina grasped this turn of events and, making up her mind in the next instant, she strode toward the exit with both hands held high before her like a shield. The pupils drew back from her as if she were a leper, and let her pass. From their massed ranks there arose, among the sighs of relief and interjections of surprise, the distinct outcry: "Look, the Devil!" echoed by "The Devil, the Devil!" from all sides. And indeed, looking at the sharp-featured, bony, noble cut of Alexina's face, with those brilliant black eyes under heavy eyebrows knit together to form an unbroken, threatening line across the bridge of her handsome nose, that outcry expressed something justifiable in the children's imagination. No sooner had Alexina disappeared from view than Henriette, who at the first moment of surprise had fled to Madame's side, was seen staring this way and that in confusion. In the grip of a similar impulse, she suddenly started to push her way through the crowd, and rushed out of the refectory.

"There goes his bride!" someone cried, followed by a chorus of "The Devil and his bride!" reiterated most vociferously by the shrill voices of the youngest, as if it were a matter of course. Now they all took their places at table, quite of their own accord, and the maids began to serve the meal. The mob had won out, and Monsieur and Madame realized for the first time what dimensions this case had assumed and what havoc had been caused in the heads of all these excitable girls by the early morning scene of the two sleepers in bed together. The sharp cries of words that seemed to be crumpled and bitten in pieces by those rows of little teeth—"the Schoolmistress" and "the Head" and "Alexina" and "the bride"—and buzzed throughout the refectory all through the meal, proved that there could be no further talk of damming this flood. Nothing less than an open, strict disciplinary treatment of the case could now save the convent and its integrity.

The meal ended, and all went their ways in a state of agitation. Monsieur and Madame, left behind, exchanged a few words. One of the upstairs maids came down to whisper a message to Madame. Meanwhile the Head was waiting at the Abbé's door. He had sent for her prior to the midday meal. She had come at the right time, he said; they must have a serious talk. They went inside together, and for a long time Monsieur paced the floor with his hands clasped behind his back. By now things had gone too far for him, too. Not only were the convent's reputation and success at stake, but the Abbé's immediate superior, the Archbishop of Rouen, might take the matter very badly indeed. Even so, the moralist and the exegetical sleuth in the Abbe were not quite laid to rest. What a splendid case! Quite medieval! If Sanchez had known of it! What would he have made of it? The shout "The Devil and his bride! The Devil and his bride!" still rang in his ears. He really had to admit it, he was rather proud of his pupils for having come up with such a fine turn of phrase.

The matter would have to be dealt with in two ways, he finally said to the Head, stopping and facing her. First, the children would have to be calmed down and their morale restored. Second, the case must be cleared up and the offenders punished, regardless of their position, and with no special consideration for the Mother Superior. The Abbé made this last point with a special emphasis, thus making the Head Sister, who was in any case a great favorite of his, into a firm ally. As for the first part of their task, the pupils were to remain in their classrooms after the end of the noon recess, and were to devote themselves to their studies. For the second part—the clarification of the baffling aspects of the case—he wanted the facts from the Head herself: Just how far had the two girls gone in their lovemaking, and how much of this indecent touching and fondling went on among young girls in general? For example, was this sort of thing ever reported in confession? Did it occur among the younger children, or also among the more mature girls, like Alexina? What did they mean by it? Was it done in response to inner promptings, or to external temptation? Et cetera, et cetera. This was a case of the greatest scientific and moral-theological significance, Monsieur added with some zeal.

The Head Sister, who was only slightly over thirty, lowered her pale face to her scapular, crossed her hands over her chest, and kept silent.

"*Mon Dieu!*" the Abbé said, becoming a little irritable. If she would not speak up, he would have to turn to the Mother Superior for the information. This had the desired effect. If Monsieur would state his questions, she conceded, she would do her best. A feasible *modus operandi*.

"Do young girls sleep together regularly?"

"Not regularly, but frequently."

"For what reason?"

"Many of the little ones are afraid to sleep alone."

"Did this lead to physical contact?"

"To the unavoidable kind of physical contact."

"Is such contact sensual in nature?"

"With the older girls, this is not to be ruled out, but the older girls do not so often sleep together."

"In such cases, would they embrace and intertwine their limbs?" Not to her personal knowledge, answered the Head, but there were always some childish and softhearted girls who might kiss and hug their friends even in the daytime, when fully clothed.

But did she, the Head Sister, regard such conduct, in some circumstances, as inspired by the Devil?

"Under no circumstances."

To what, then, did she attribute it?

"Character, temperament."

"Are these not tainted by Original Sin?"

"Certainly. But to distinguish between the human and the devilish element in our natures must be left to the wisdom of Monsieur; it is beyond me."

"Is it fairly common for girls to put a hand under each other's skirts?"

"A hand, no, but they do look."

"But that's impossible!"

"Not with the little ones who still wear short skirts; when they walk up the stairs, for instance."

"What do they have in mind?"

"Curiosity, to see what their classmates are wearing, whether they keep their linen clean or not. They love to carry tales about each other. If Cecile, for example, notices a torn slip or a run in Claire's stocking, she may tell her friends that Claire's petticoats are in rags, that she wears torn stockings. If this gets back to Claire, she tells everyone that Cecile is always looking under everybody's skirts. That's how girls are, tattletales."

"Do the older girls, like Alexina and Henriette, also go in for this sort of thing?"

"In a different way. They would be motivated by their concern with dressing well."

"Does this lead to their touching each other?"

"Only in the inevitable way."

"Is the touching of another girl's body intentional, at such times?"

"Many girls like to boast of their beauty, the perfection of their figures. Their listeners become interested in seeing for themselves, and this leads to mutual inspections."

"Do you believe that the girls are prompted by the Devil in such doings?"

This was not for her to say! Besides, on such occasions the girls were still dressed in the flannels, shirting, muslins of their underclothes.

"But muslin, tulle, gauze is the kind of stuff the Devil finds most to his taste!"

"In that case, there is great danger," murmured the Head, "since Henriette has such an abundance of rich and luxurious clothing."

With this, the conversation came to an end. The Abbé found himself no wiser than before. What he really wanted to know—namely whether Henriette and Alexina were drawn to each other by a diabolic sensuality, something more or less in the area of tribadism, or whether they had merely gone too far in expressing a passionate friendship based on a spiritual affinity—was something the Head could not tell him, since she herself did not know, and in any case this sort of experience was so rare. However, in the first case, Monsieur's mind was made up that the Schoolmistress would have to be dismissed, regardless of her excellent qualifications in other respects, and that Henriette would have to be sent away. In the second case, a simple reprimand would do.

Meanwhile Henriette and Alexina had stayed upstairs with Madame, where the conversation had been no less intense. For her afternoon coffee the Mother Superior came down to the Abbé. She declared that something would have to be done to save the convent's name among the country's noble families. It was simple enough to confiscate outgoing letters, but on Sundays, when the parents came to take their daughters for an outing, the story was bound to leak, to be blown up and otherwise distorted. Monsieur discoursed on his moral-theological distinctions and scruples, upon which the outcome of the case solely depended. To this the Mother Superior replied with some acerbity that the world outside was no more likely than she to understand such scholarly hairsplitting. It was necessary first of all to cut off all further talk, to which end she proposed to send the two girls away for a while.

The Abbé firmly disagreed. To do what she proposed would be to admit to a disgrace before it had been proven. He would like, in any case, to interrogate Alexina. By all means, Madame said sourly. Meanwhile she intended to remove her niece from any further insults by lodging her, for the time being, at the parish priest's. So saying, she quit the Abbé's room without waiting for an answer.

A few minutes later the Schoolmistress, with eyes red from weeping, entered the Abbé's room, cast herself down at his feet, and began to sob.

"Ah, Mademoiselle," the Abbé began, "you have already done great, incalculably great moral damage to the convent, and I fear that you have an even greater sin upon your conscience."

"*Mon Père*," Alexina broke in, putting special emphasis on these words and looking up at him with great, shining eyes. "My love for Henriette is pure as the snows of Mount Hebron; my feelings for her are like doves, that know no evil!"

This kind of language took the Abbé off his guard. Nor was he, in his exalted way, insensitive to poetic turns of phrase. All the same, such grandiloquent protestations, after all the unsavory revelations of the day, struck a painfully false note. He could not refrain from countering with: "And what about the way you two fondle each other, and embrace, and explore each other's bodies, then?"

"Ah, *mon Père*," Alexina again intoned, "it is true, I did admire Henriette's appearance, her body, her hair, her eyes, her voice, her walk; everything, in short; her stockings, her shoes, all she was and all she wore; because I myself am nothing, and have nothing, and look like nothing. And Henriette, I think, felt the same kind of admiration for my spirit, my energy, my learning, what little something I have from God: my soul. We did indeed touch one another wherever we could, however it was possible. She touched my soul; I, her body; yes, we did, with a fervor, *mon Père*. Which no two girls have ever felt for one another; such fervor, *mon Père*, is surely permitted in friendship, in love, as it is in prayer, in remorse, in devotion to God."

Here the Abbé was really overwhelmed—this girl was too much for him. "And did no base, improper feelings, or sinful desires ever enter your soul, my daughter?" he insisted.

"Only enthusiasm," Alexina cried, stretching both arms upward in a transport, "only the enthusiasm God Himself has planted in our souls."

"Very well," the Abbé said, lifting the girl, who had been on her knees before him all this time, to her feet. "Very well, let us hope that it will all turn out for the best. May God keep your soul from harm in future, too." Alexina went back upstairs to Madame, and everything seemed to have taken a turn for the better.

However, at about four o'clock the Head came down, bringing a packet of letters taken from Henriette, who had been caught trying to smuggle it out of her desk drawer to take along to the parish priest's house. The handwriting was Alexina's, so the letters could be expected to contribute something toward the clarification of the girls' relationship. Monsieur opened the letters and began to read, and went on reading, quite losing himself in the reading of them. He read these letters as he read Liguori or the Church Fathers. Monsieur was much too subtle, too well schooled, too much a classicist and too spiritual a man not to recognize the precious attar that rose from these impassioned letters, not to feel inebriated by it. So this was the good French style for which Alexina was so much admired, which constituted her foremost qualification as a teacher, if not as a writer. It was out of these passionate effusions that it had crystallized, out of an ultimately worldly affection. Yet Alexina was constantly invoking God! One of the letters contained the following passage:

So you want to escape from me, Henriette. It frightens you when you see my eyes grow dim, when you hear my voice grow dry. Don't you know that it's too late? Don't you know that you have been given into my hands, like wax in the hands of a sculptor? That you must love the unhappy Alexina, because you are so rich and I am so poor? Do you fear God? Have you no fear of becoming desperately unhappy if you turn away the poor village girl, Alexina, whom you love, and who adores you? Don't we, together, have everything? Doesn't each of us, apart, have nothing at all? Do you see my thin, feeble arms? Well then, your arms, so voluptuous, make up for it. Stroking my thin body, you find my breasts flat. But you, bursting with life, have breasts swelling with milk and blood! What if you measure my legs and find only bony crutches, childlike and weak? Don't you have thighs like marble columns, and knees dainty as the eggs of a partridge? Your soul is often asleep, and your memory retains nothing. But haven't I great strength of soul, and don't I know you and myself by heart? You are behind in your studies, and your words are those of a child. Am I not far ahead of the rest, and haven't I carried you with me? Aren't you the dove, and I the hawk who comes down on you like a thunderbolt? Aren't you in my power? And yet you fear me, who alone can save you? Do you intend to throw yourself into the bestial arms of a man, where you can find nothing but brutality, obscenity, and vulgarity? Aren't I your husband? . . .

In another letter, she had written:

"You avoid me; then you come looking for me again. You tell me that I am different from all the other girls here at the convent, and that you ought to loathe me because I make you do things, and do you violence, such as a nice girl should not put up with; and then you have to give in to me, after all. The precepts of the cloister, Henriette, and the so-called rules of decorum, cannot set the measure, define the bounds, of what we feel. The wrong we have done, touching each other, those forbidden kisses and embraces and effusions, and the things we did in secret, all that doesn't matter in itself; it's not what this is really all about. It's only symbolic of what we could not express in words—just as folding your hands as in prayer is only a symbolic gesture for what we feel in our hearts. What is behind all this is something else entirely, something inexpressible. What we feel, you and I, Henriette, when we look at each other, or think of each other, is something inexpressible. Compared with this, whatever we might do that is against the rules doesn't matter. It is only a form of expression, a kind of explosion, which might have taken some other form, but simply happens to have taken this form. Your love for me, Henriette, is all that matters to me. If you are sure of it, then hold me fast, I will take care of you. . . .

In a third letter, he read:

Where do babies come from? We know all about that now, thanks to my telling you. But doesn't everything connected with it, everything that leads up to it, add up to filth, stink, vomit, vulgar heavy breathing and staring, all manner of vileness? Here, everything that is done outwardly is revolting, and the inward divine sentiment minimal. What we do with each other,

Henriette, is always gentle, delicate, playful, insubstantial, while our inward feelings, the divine impulse behind it, is immense! With my inner being I could take in the whole world, surround it, absorb it into myself! And you, Henriette, are only a little, unspeakably beautiful figurine-image of this world; one little shimmering fish in the vast ocean! . . .

As he read on, the clock struck five. The Abbé was well aware that he had an extraordinary case on his hands, an event, a relationship that went back many months, ripening slowly, like a wasp's nest growing cell by cell until a huge hive had formed. Here the Schoolmistress had undoubtedly played the role of master-builder, creator, aggressor, while Henriette played a more passive role. But Monsieur was not yet certain just how far the erotic life of the two girls had gone physically, though Alexina's letters so exuberantly and rapturously expressed its spiritual side. Surely the possibility that this might be a most ingenious, well-camouflaged maneuver by the Devil himself could not be ignored? That Alexina was a naïve, if impetuous, creature who regarded the authenticity of her feelings as a sufficient justification for her conduct, but was still basically unspoiled, he had no doubt whatever. But what now? He could not make up his mind about the proper punishment—warning, expulsion, or separation of the two girls. He could not decide whether he would have to sacrifice such brilliant gifts, in the person of Alexina.

It was now time for vespers. The girls were allowed half an hour of recreation before the two hours of study which concluded the day's work. There was a great ferment and buzzing among the young creatures, who had been warned to trouble the Abbé no further with their observations and opinions. Thus they were that much busier taking counsel and exchanging ideas among themselves or with their actual confidantes, the nuns. The removal of Henriette to the parish priest's house was taken as a confirmation that they had been on the right track. But it was also known that the Schoolmistress, who was regarded by all the girls as the real instigator of the affair, was still closeted upstairs with Madame. So all the talk and speculation was again concentrated upon her person. Even worse than this, in consequence of Henriette's move to the village, the folk of Beauregard had been drawn into the discussion, and they too found ways to add new fuel to the fire. As a result, one of the servants was knocking at the Abbé's door at about five-thirty, the end of the recess, and was admitted, together with the Head, who had encouraged her to make the following report: On her way back from taking Henriette to His Reverence in the village, and delivering Madame's letter, several of the villagers had clustered around her, suggesting how much they already knew about the extraordinary events at the cloister. Realizing that there was no secret to be kept any longer, she had admitted the known facts and talked with the people. Almost all of them seemed to feel that *la belle Henriette*, as they called her, was quite a good, decent girl, whereas Mademoiselle Alexina, with her tall stride, bony shoulders, hollow voice, sunken cheeks, and those grown-together eyebrows was a decidedly suspect character. Please the Lord to protect the convent from the likes of her. Then a hulking sunburned fellow stepped forward. He had a big beard on his cheeks and chin and an axe on his shoulder, and had been there listening hard all along. He told them that about six weeks before, on one of his walks of inspection through the woods—he was a forester—he had heard moans deep inside the thicket, some distance from the road. Approaching the spot, not without cracking a few twigs and such, so the noise might have given him away, he kept hearing a high, whimpering female voice, alternating with a deep, resonant, reassuring male voice. When finally he parted the last branches in his way, he was surprised to find two girls who had only just risen up from lying under the bushes. The one with the high voice must have lain underneath the other, as she was slower in getting to her feet. The one with the deep voice was already standing, but it was evident from her posture and the markings on the ground that she had *not* lain *beside* her friend; they had not yet succeeded in pulling their dresses down to cover the exposed lower parts of their bodies, and so he also noticed that the taller, slimmer one's legs had a thick growth of black hair on them. They both ran off, and he did not follow them. All those present, including the maid, had then asked the warden to stay in the vicinity, in case Monsieur l'Abbé wished to speak with him. The rest was up to Monsieur.

After listening to this story, the Abbé dismissed the maid in order to have a word with the Head in private. After a mere twenty minutes, during which Monsieur translated for her some passages in various Latin and French books, another nun entered the room in a state of evident dismay, saying that a crowd of several hundred people had gathered at the gate, armed with pitchforks and axes, shaking their fists at the cloister, cursing aloud and insisting that the Devil was being harbored in the convent.

Faced with this new development, the Abbé was hesitant, then ordered the nun who had brought him the news to report it to the Mother Superior and to request that lady to come down. Turning to the Head, he suggested that it might be a good idea to let the forest warden come in, to pacify the mob. But just outside the convent portals, as she was about to execute this mission, the Head ran into the parish priest in haste to see Monsieur. She took His Reverence in to the Abbé and listened as the priest asked what on earth was going on. Half the village was gathered in front of his house, with a tale of an incubus—unless it was the Devil himself—who had raped or tried to rape the lovely Henriette, Madame's niece, in the woods. This devil had taken the shape of one of the teachers at the convent, the one known as the Schoolmistress. The villagers had come to beg the priest to hurry to see the Abbé at the convent, so that the teacher would be made to confess and the demon could be exorcised.

The Abbé was briefing his colleague on the events of the day while the girls were heard racing up and down the stairs outside with piercing cries of "The Devil and his bride! The Devil and his bride!" while others recited in rhythmic unison a doggerel composed for the occasion:

> The Devil must hide
> in fear and distress!
> He has lost his bride
> and deceived the Abbess!

Soon Madame came in, trembling with shock. The girls had come storming out of their classrooms as if on signal, screaming that the Devil was loose inside the convent, and determined to drag Alexina out of the Mother Superior's apartment. She was now convinced that the whole thing was a plot directed against herself, the Mother Superior; the Devil had little to do with it. The two clerics looked doubtful. But there was a simple way to put an immediate end to all this nonsense, Madame went on—simply get the village doctor to come and examine Alexina in Madame's presence, in her apartment upstairs. If the well-known marks and stigmata of diabolic possession were found on the girl's body, which Madame was inclined to doubt very much, further steps could be taken—if necessary, exorcism. If Alexina were found to be *virgo intacta*, without any such stigma, as Madame confidently expected, then the persons who had deliberately spawned and spread such a tale must be properly punished.

This suggestion met with full agreement. Just one thing, the parish priest said: if the warden who was haranguing the villagers outside could be given an opportunity to see Alexina, unbeknownst to her, his impartial testimony—providing he did not identify her as the culprit he had seen— might lead to a quick pacification of the mobs inside and outside the cloister. This proposal also met with general acclaim. As for the young boarders, they were ordered to keep still in the refectory, under the nuns' supervision, until the results of the medical examination were known.

It was now seven o'clock in the evening. During the preceding two hours the Devil had indeed been on the loose, with all order and discipline gone in the convent. The plan about to be undertaken had a reassuring effect on all those present. The priest went back to the village church for his monstrance and ciborium. On the way he had a soothing word for all the people he met. In addition, twilight was setting in, and the majority started to go home. While the Head Sister went to fetch the physician, Madame prepared what was necessary for his reception upstairs. Monsieur had sent word to his sacristan to have everything in readiness for an exorcism, and set about looking up all the special directives to be followed, turning to Bodin's *Demono-mania* for the physical stigmata of a covenant with the Devil. The girls were given their supper in the refectory. Nightfall had subdued their boisterousness, which slowly gave place to apprehensiveness and fear. All of them pleaded to have the lights left on in the dormitories. Meanwhile the woodsman had returned downstairs to assure the Abbé, beyond any doubt, that the girl he had just watched through a crack in the door—sitting in Mother Superior's room, red-eyed from weeping—was indeed the incubus he had seen with Henriette in the woods.

It was already half past eight when the physician, a young man with a distinguished degree from the medical faculty of Paris, arrived at the convent. He had been on a call in a neighboring village, and upon his return had heard the whole peculiar story. The lights were already on at the convent, and the deepest silence reigned in the halls and stairwells. The doctor declined the Abbé's proposal to begin by going over Bodin's list of stigmata. Instead he was immediately ac-companied upstairs by the Head Sister. Madame received him with every mark of civility in the brilliantly lit, richly appointed salon of her suite. A single lamp was lit in the adjoining room, seen through the half-open door, where Alexina, crouching partly undressed on the edge of the bed, awaited the doctor. After a few words to Madame, he went inside, closing the door, not quite completely, with a casual movement of his hand. Despite Madame's efforts to insulate herself by noisily turning the pages of her book, the following sounds could be heard: a brief murmur and the formulas of greeting; a series of terse questions, tersely answered. Both voices were deep, but the doctor's voice came through a shade higher, more sharply, while Alexina's had a duller, more throaty timbre. The lamp was moved so that all the light was gone from the minimal opening of the door. A directive was given, followed by the sounds of garments being slipped off. There was a pause, followed by another order and a reply. The order was repeated more firmly; a sigh, and the sounds of more clothing being pulled off, sounds of slipping, of someone stamping on the floor in stockinged feet, once, then again, and again; another sliding sound, and then a soft, slippery gliding, like skin on skin, accompanied by an encouraging: "Yes, that's it, that's it, fine," from the doctor. A long pause, then another order; the bed creaking, then the sound of a body slipping onto a mattress; a quiet request, repeated more firmly, followed by an urgent, impatient command. The response was a sigh and whimper, "Ah, you're hurting me, Monsieur." Then Alexina suddenly cried out, loudly and explosively. There was an indistinct reply from the doctor, whose uneven breathing suggested that he was concentrating hard, meeting with difficulty. Alexina sobbed without restraint, not crying out with pain, but weeping in total self-abandonment, powerless, despairing. The doctor's voice became gentle, compassionate, without further commands. The worst seemed to be over, the question resolved, but the outcome seemed to be a sad one. Even so, it took quite a while before the examination was fully concluded. At Alexina's cry of fear, Madame had ceased leafing through the book and had begun to listen intently, holding her breath and staring hard at the crack in the door, as the whimpering inside grew gradually more feeble. Finally the weeping turned into a rhythmic lament, synchronous with the patient's breathing. At last, after a long time—almost an hour had passed—there was the sound of water being poured into a basin. Soon thereafter the doctor emerged, with a troubled face, holding a hand towel. The Mother Superior stood up and looked at him questioningly.

"A sad case, Madame," the doctor said darkly. "I shall have to write out a detailed report, which I hope to be able to deliver to the Abbé sometime in the morning. Meanwhile I would suggest that you send young Alexina as soon as possible—it's probably too late for tonight—to the priest's house. Bring Mademoiselle Henriette back here." With this, the doctor took his leave, told the sacristan, who was waiting in the hall, that there was no occasion for any kind of religious ceremony, and went home, away from the now deathly silence of the convent.

The time was now eleven, and everyone was in bed, though wide awake, for who could sleep after such a day? Upstairs the sisters slipped lightly from bed to bed in their long white nightgowns, and quieted the little girls and their terrors. All the lamps burned brightly. The Head Sister went in person from one dorm to another, to make sure that there would be no further disorder, no new outbreak of panic. She knew that she had won her game.

Downstairs, Monsieur l'Abbé lay awake in his bed. He had received the message that there was no need to set an exorcism in motion, had ordered the sacristan, who brought it, to pass the word to the village priest, and had gone to bed, after a few words with the Head to make sure that it would be a peaceful night. No need to take recourse to exorcism, indeed! Did these young doctors imagine they could keep the world in order without any help from the clergy? And if there were no stigmata, then what was wrong with

Alexina? If the Devil had used her phantom, her physical envelope, then according to all the medieval exorcists he could not have done so without leaving physical marks on it. If, on the other hand, the Devil was not involved at all, then Henriette and the Schoolmistress had evidently been playing a most heinous, sinful game with one another. How could they do such unsavory things in the woods? Even if there was no one else to see but themselves? Ah yes, he remembered now. Henriette had more than once this spring obtained special permission from Madame to go to the woods with Alexina in the afternoon to pick lilies-of-the-valley. One time he had seen her on her return with bunches of flowers and feverishly glistening eyes. But what now, with the Schoolmistress found to be free of stigmata? He did not know what to make of it. They were apparently back where they started from. In the end, it would still be up to the clerisy to resolve the matter. Such were the thoughts coursing through the Abbé's mind.

Up on the second floor, Madame was resting. She had grave misgivings about her future as prioress. Since six o'clock this evening, when the peasants had stood at the gate waving their scythes, looking for the Devil in the person of a teacher inside the convent, it was clear to her that she would have to bear the brunt of this. The Head Sister had played her game well this time. A flame, that could have been extinguished this morning, had been fueled at the right moment, and had turned into a conflagration. Good Lord, two young girls whose physical and spiritual qualities happened to complement one another, found in bed together, full of mutual tenderness! What of it? Alexina was an odd creature, to be sure, and the doctor's few words indicated that there must be something special the matter with her. . . .

In the adjoining room, Alexina lay on her bed. Only yesterday she was universally admired, praised for her phenomenal intellectual powers, called the Schoolmistress in homage. She knew that the little girls had felt honored when she spoke to them. Now she was a whimpering creature, mortally wounded. Her most intimate secrets were about to be exposed to all the world by a doctor. She would be pilloried as a female incarnation of Satan, and robbed of Henriette, the wellspring of her life. This evening, when the doctor was with her, she had realized that something out of the ordinary was indeed the matter with her. When he examined her from head to toe, measuring and testing everything; when he probed her even in those private parts everyone hid in shame, and caused her such cruel pain that she had to cry aloud; when he tried to penetrate that secret place, and she saw his puzzled expression, she started to wonder what it could be. She had known, of course, that she was made somewhat differently from the other girls, such as Henriette, but she had never given it much thought —wasn't everybody different in one way or another? One girl might have a beak of a nose, another a snub nose, and still another a straight one. One would have an ugly, fleshy mouth; another would have finely drawn lips like a sculpture; one girl might have a flat chest, another a rounded bust; one would be stupid, another would have a fine mind. So what was all the fuss about, where she was concerned? Was it that little thing that made Henriette laugh every time? If it wasn't that, then why the terrible painfulness there? And so the poor creature went on whimpering and brooding and sobbing.

The vast cloak of night still covered everything: the convent, its inmates, and their thoughts. But the sun was already aflame with ardor, ready to break through and light up the whole dreadful affair at the cloister, to burn it in letters of fire on everyone's brain, everyone's conscience.

Once more it was seven in the morning, and the sun shone through the window panes of the Abbé's study. The breakfast dishes had been pushed to one side of the work table, and Monsieur was again reading intently in Liguori, *Theologiae moralis, libri sex*. Nothing in his face gave a hint of uneasiness or fatigue. The previous day's incidents had left no trace of nervousness in him. His features were composed and serene, as they had been on the previous morning.

There was a knock at the door. "Come in," Monsieur said, and the concierge brought in a large envelope, just delivered. Monsieur slit it open at the corner, unfolded the heavy sheet of paper and read the following:

Beauregard, 21 June 1831

Adolphe Duval, physician, diplomate of the Medical Faculty of Paris, to Monsieur l'Abbé de Rochechouard, Douay.

Monsieur: I have the honor to report the following findings with regard to the physical condition of the so-called Alexina Besnard, eighteen years of age, as the result of my examination of the above named yesterday evening:

Alexina is exceptionally tall for a girl, and would be considered tall, even for a man. Her thin face shows keen intelligence; her glance is decidedly masculine; prominent eyebrows overshadow quick, clever eyes. There is no trace of a beard; the hair on the head is longer than generally worn by men, but far from reaching the length of a girl's hair (unless it has been deliberately cut). It is worn in a snood, though it is not very abundant. Alexina's voice is an alto. The physique is slender, muscular, lacking in fatty deposits, feminine in the upper part, with a fine skin, and undeveloped mammaries with nipples which are female in structure. The lower extremities are noticeably covered with a thick, dark, masculine growth of hair and also tend toward a masculine configuration. The upper thighs are straight rather than showing the typically female convergence toward the knees. The hands are small, but the feet are notably large and strong. The hips, by their general appearance, the total absence of lateral curvature, as well as by measurements, must be described as constituting a pelvic structure of masculine type. The *mons veneris* is covered with a thick growth of hair which at first glance obscures the actual form of the genitalia. These consist of fleshy *labia majora* folded over the small, underdeveloped *labia minora*; there is no trace of a hymen. The *introitus vagina* is so tight, and any effort to penetrate it causes such pain, that there can be no doubt of its ending in a *cul de sac*, giving no access to a uterus unless it were, at most, a quite rudimentary one, unlikely to involve ovulation or menstruation. On the other hand, the *labia minora* enclose, in the upper part, a succulent body, perforated at the tip, which proves to be a well-defined *membrum virile*, capable of erection, although its full development is inhibited by a firm ligament attaching it, on its underside, to the above-named lesser labia. The perforation is the orifice permitting the urethra, which leads into the *vesica urinalis*, or bladder, to discharge the contents of same. There are no testicles in evidence; they appear to have remained, undescended, in the abdominal cavity.

Such being the case, Alexina Besnard is a hermaphrodite and, inasmuch as he had, in the course of the examination, evidently as a result of a momentary physical excitation, an involuntary emission of semen, which proved under the microscope to contain normal, mobile spermatozoa, Alexina must be regarded as a male hermaphrodite. Alexina is, in fact, a *man*, and indeed a man capable of procreation.

It is accordingly my duty to notify the authorities at Alexina's birthplace to correct the records to that effect, and I have already done so, leaving it to Your Reverence to take any further steps to secure the definitive official correction of the record with regard to the civil status of Alexina Besnard.

Yours most respectfully,
Adolphe Duval.

. . . . .

That same day Alexina was returned to her village and her parents.

Mademoiselle Henriette de Bujac, who returned to the convent, found it necessary to leave it again after about six months, for the home of an aunt in a distant part of the country. Madame de Vremy took her departure from the convent at Douay at the same time. She was succeeded as Mother Superior by the former Head Sister.

"A Scandal at the Convent"
Translated from the German, "Ein Skandalöser Fall," by Sophie Wilkins.

• • • • •

Herculine Barbin was a French hermaphrodite. Designated female at birth in 1838 and raised as a girl in religious institutions, she was redesignated male when she was twenty-two.

Michel Foucault holds a chair at the Collège de France, the most prestigious academic institution in that country. His latest book is the highly acclaimed *History of Sexuality*. He is also the author of *Madness and Civilization* and *Discipline and Punish*.

Richard McDougall is a writer and translator. His most recent work is a translation of *The Very Rich Hours of Adrienne Monnier*.

"A Scandal at the Convent" was written in 1893 by Oscar Panizza. The story was translated from the German, *Ein Skandalöser Fall*, by Sophie Wilkins.

• • • • •